Praise for *You Are Driving Me Crazy!*

"June Bratcher, the owner-operator of Daisy Tours, has written a most interesting book regarding her newest volume, *You're Driving Me Crazy!*. From the early days of her beginnings as a bus owner, Mrs. Bratcher has literally lived the motor coach business. She is the owner of a fleet of twenty-six beautiful motor coaches, all mostly Van Hools manufactured in Belgium. Her company enjoys an enviable reputation in the tours and travel business. Her drivers are excellent, and the Daisy Tours guides are among the best informed historians in the city of San Antonio."

—**Docia Williams**, Author

"June Bratcher has set a wonderful example of an entrepreneurial woman, but at the same time has shown caring for her community in giving services and assistance. She has earned respect and admiration from all who have had the opportunity to work with her and know her as a friend."

—**Lila Cockrell**, Mayor Emeritus, San Antonio

"June Bratcher dared to dream and make dreams come true for all of us."

—**Belle Chenault**, American Medical Association

"Because of her passion for the industry and her compassion for people, June has become a huge asset to the motor coach industry as well as the San Antonio community. Her leadership has provided both with knowledge and innovation. For almost two decades, I have cherished June as a client and a friend."

—**Greg Gates**, Senior Account Manager, ABC Companies

YOU ARE DRIVING ME CRAZY!

June Bratcher

ARCHWAY
PUBLISHING

Archway Publishing books may be ordered through booksellers or by contacting:

Archway Publishing
1663 Liberty Drive
Bloomington, IN 47403
www.archwaypublishing.com
1 (888) 242-5904

Because of the dynamic nature of the Internet, any web addresses or
links contained in this book may have changed since publication and may
no longer be valid. The views expressed in this work are solely those
of the author and do not necessarily reflect the views of the publisher,
and the publisher hereby disclaims any responsibility for them.

Any people depicted in stock imagery provided by Thinkstock are models,
and such images are being used for illustrative purposes only.
Certain stock imagery © Thinkstock.

ISBN: 978-1-4808-2818-6 (sc)
ISBN: 978-1-4808-2819-3 (hc)
ISBN: 978-1-4808-2820-9 (e)

Library of Congress Control Number: 2016907223

Print information available on the last page.

Archway Publishing rev. date: 07/18/2016

"Whatever women do they must do twice as well as a man to be thought half as good; luckily this is not difficult." - Charlotte Whitton

That is a quote on an engraved stone plaque my husband gave me on the day I started my company. September 8, 1980

After more than 35 years – I agree! It is not difficult.

June Bratcher

Dedicated To My Children

Beth Clegg
Kim Kuykendall
Daniel Bratcher
David Bratcher

I would like to thank my editor.
Sheryl L. Harley
sherylharley@gmail.com

June Bratcher with her children, from left to right, Kim Kuykendall, David Bratcher, Daniel Bratcher, June Bratcher, and Beth Clegg.

Background

I was born in Andover, Ohio, a small northeastern Ohio village that borders Pennsylvania and the shores of Pymatuning Lake. Winters were long and cold for our farming family. My father, John, farmed the land. My mother, Clara, worked in a grocery store. If we were poor, we children did not realize it. The farm kept us going. Our small house had what they called four rooms and a path. The path was to the outhouse. A bathroom was not put in until after I went to nursing school.

I wanted very much to get off the farm. My pathway to do that was to go to nursing school. Our family did not have the money to send me to Cleveland for the training, so I applied and was awarded a full scholarship. The only problem was that I needed $65 to purchase the uniforms I would need. The summer before I was to go, I worked in the local grocery store. Mom sold homemade bread and cookies to people from Cleveland who had come to Andover to fish at Pymatuning Lake. Together we earned the $65 I needed. Fifty-six students started in my class. Twenty-nine graduated, and I was one of them. That day in September of 1953 was a great day for the whole family.

During my last year in training, I met a young pre-med student named Everett Bratcher from Ohio State University. We were married the fall after I graduated, now that I could support him. I spent the next 9 years putting Everett through medical school, internship, and surgical residency. Later, with my husband's education completed and my children grown, I was ready to do something just for myself. At the age of 48, I became an entrepreneur, and with $200 saved from grocery money, I set out on my journey.

This is the story of my journey to a $5.75 million company.

Contents

Preface

The Struggle of the Early Years

As I look back at the early years, I wonder how I thought I could ever make it. There were so many close calls. There were so many people telling me to give up. I marvel that I always found a way to persevere. There were days I thought, "If I can make it through the next 2 or 3 days, I will be okay." I expected setbacks, but I was determined that if I failed I would just go back to nursing. That way I could pay off my debts and start over. I knew success would not come overnight. I had to be in this for the long haul, and I was totally committed.

A huge problem at the start was the cost of the buses. My first 7 years, I leased buses from a local bus company. Then the law changed, and I was required to own a bus if I wanted to lease it for profit. Now I had to own a bus of some kind. I shopped around and found an old city-type bus and was able to buy it for $1,400 on a payment plan. I parked it behind our office building, and when authorities came and asked where my bus was, I pointed to my old inner city bus on our lot. They were satisfied. I never intended to use it. It was only symbolic, but it allowed me to lease good buses from local bus companies.

Then a strange thing happened. People came to our office asking if they could rent that bus to go to the zoo or children's museums. It was a plain vanilla bus with hard seats and no frills.

But, it ran very well. Schools needing economy transportation started using it, and it really paid off. It was enough to pay the rent each month. My first bus--it was already making a profit.

Success can come from small, unexpected places.

Our first outbound trip was to an herb farm in east Texas. I planned the whole thing right down to every last detail. It had a getaway breakfast and tour of the herb farm, followed by lunch and a class on cooking with herbs. I advertised in the newspaper, and we had a sellout crowd. I got a guide to help me, as I wanted everything to go perfectly, and it did. "Wow," I thought, "this is hard and it is a lot of work, but we made our first outbound trip profitable." Now I was absolutely sure I could make it, but soon I learned future trips would not always turn out so well.

I had to determine what would sell and what would make a trip worthwhile. I had to find people who liked the trips and how much they could afford to pay. I learned quickly not to buy tickets that might not sell, as I could not give them back for a refund.

I had to learn the seasons, like Spring Break for schools and colleges, high school track and field, professional football teams' schedules, as well as those for other football teams. I needed to approach all of them and offer our services. I was building a base, and it was slow work.

There were other things to take care of. We needed an address other than my home. I didn't like asking clients to come to my house for information or to sign a contract. I found a very small two-room office in a high-rise building close to my house. It was small, but at least it was a business address and something I could afford. I looked for clients who needed coaches on a regular basis. It would guarantee that I could pay the rent. Instead of trying to sell a trip to a game for a high school football game, I tried to get the entire schedule. I found that giving them service beyond their expectations worked well. Therefore, once I booked a trip, I went the extra mile. I confirmed everything the day before, giving them the name of their driver and his or her phone number as well as my cell phone number. The day of the trip, I showed up 30 minutes early, which made the customer comfortable knowing the bus would be on time. Lastly, I paid the driver to show up 20 to 30 minutes early just to impress them.

I had to teach my drivers that being even 5 minutes late to a pick-up point seemed like nothing to them, but it was a lifetime to a client who had 40 to 50 people waiting at the curb not knowing if the bus would ever come. It paid off. My clients knew they could depend on me, and it began to load my base as well as my bottom line. I wanted to impress them so much they would not think of going elsewhere. To this day, I do my best to keep my base strong. If I lose a big account, the whole staff works on replacing it. It is my comfort zone, and I protect it with a vengeance.

I did not have the funds to advertise, so I looked for free opportunities. Surprisingly there were a lot. I went to every grand opening I could find. I offered to help with community service projects that needed volunteers. I got involved with political candidates who needed volunteers. I did anything to get my name out there.

It took some time for the transportation community to accept that a woman might own a bus company. I had to prove myself repeatedly. It was okay. I didn't mind. I understood. It took almost 3 years before they accepted me. When they learned that I had a pilot license, that seemed to impress them, and I became "one of the guys."

Getting a Real Bus

As I worked getting my company stable, owning my own coach was always on my mind. There had to be a way. At this time, women were not allowed to sign their own name to a loan without a co-signer. Asking my husband or my 18-year-old son to sign for me was out of the question. They were willing, but I was not. I considered it humiliating. I had to find a way that I could sign my own name on a loan.

I had been working with many other women's organizations that were in the same boat. Then the Equal Credit Opportunity Act was finally passed, but some banks still didn't honor it. No longer did banks say women couldn't sign because it was against the law, because the law said we could. Their solution was to say that it was the "bank policy" that women couldn't sign. I had to find a bank without that particular policy.

I set out to find a bank or bus company that would take a chance and lend me enough to buy one bus. It could even be a used bus, but I wanted one I could be proud of and that was reliable. As a last resort, I started calling on bus companies who sold new and used coaches. I contacted ABC Companies (ABC) in Dallas. They sold Van Hool buses, built in Belgium, and had both new and used coaches. I liked their company, but they had nothing to offer me.

A few days after my visit, I got a call from a salesman, Greg Gates, at ABC. He said he had an idea and asked if he could come see me. "Absolutely. Name the day!" I responded. He came to my office the next day. I was all ears. "There is a plan," he said. "It's called lease to buy. It doesn't require a lot down because you are just leasing the bus, but at the end of the lease you have the option to buy and get some credit for all of your payments."

This was my big chance, and I went for it. I would be working with their representative, and he made all of the arrangements.

At last, I would have a coach, a new coach. I couldn't ask for more. I never missed a payment, and at the end I was able to purchase it. I bought my next three coaches in the "lease-to-own plan." It was perfect for me, and I signed my own name to the deal. For the next 25 years, all of my coaches were Van Hool, and they still are today. I am a very loyal customer. Other bus companies come to my office now wanting to sell me coaches. I tell them, "Where were you when I needed you?"

I have 26 coaches now, worth more than $6 million. In 2014, I purchased 10 new Van Hools, but there was a difference. I had 10 coaches to trade in, and that really helped. I never missed or was late with a payment. The association I have now with ABC is more like a family than a customer. They look out for me and take wonderful care of my fleet. We have been to the Van Hool plant in Belgium, and because of our loyalty, they treat us like royalty. They are always there when I need them. I feel lucky to have them, and Daisy Charters and Shuttles is fiercely loyal because ABC and Van Hool deserve it.

Chapter 1

The Early Years

I never planned to be one of the few woman-owned bus companies in America. I dreamed of doing well, but never ever of owning a $5.75 million company. I am a registered nurse (RN) by profession, and I use those skills every day with my family, friends, neighbors, and especially my bus company employees. I was not one of those women who always wanted to be a nurse. When I grew up in the 1940s, a girl could be a nurse, a teacher, or a housewife. I chose to become a nurse. It would get me out of that small town, and I wanted so badly to go to a big city.

My RN served me well. I graduated in September of 1953, and I got married the same month to a pre-med student, Everett Bratcher. I spent the next 9 years taking care of our house, home, and children and working to put him through medical school, internship, and surgical residency.

After a stint in the Air Force, Everett graduated in 1963 as a doctor specializing in surgery. Well, I know things happen to husbands. I also knew I wanted more than RN after my name, but how could I start over?

I was good at cooking, not gourmet, but more like country cooking and baking. During the Great Depression, my dad had been a baker earning $25 a week. That was good money then.

He made enough to buy a small farm. He taught my sisters and me how to bake bread, cookies, pies, and cakes, and we were good at it.

Our mom taught us how to do other things. We raised a garden, harvested fruit from the orchard, and canned foods for the winter. She worked full time, so meals were always up to us girls. We even had to cook for the threshers who came to help harvest the wheat. My sisters and I shared in preparing the meals. One of us would prepare the four or five meats, one of us the vegetables, and one of us the bread and dessert. We set everything up in the yard for 25 to 30 harvesters. I always wanted to do the dessert. Five pies, four cakes, four-dozen cookies, and there was never anything left over. One nice surprise was that sometimes a thresher would leave a dime or a quarter under his plate. We divided any money that the threshers left. What a treat!

I had learned a lot about cooking, which is what made me good at it. So when Everett started his practice, I figured my forte was cooking. I had a friend, Lenny Angel, who liked cooking, and we decided to start a cooking school. First, we wrote a small cookbook called *Let Us Entertain You*. We used it to teach from and, to our surprise, it was also selling very well in local bookstores. We were in our third printing when we decided to branch out.

Our idea was to take our students to well-known restaurants. On the bus on the way to restaurants, we would serve appetizers and go over the dinner menu planned for that evening. Going home, we would serve desserts and give them recipes for everything we had eaten. Our students loved it!

It was going well. We had many excursions and a waiting list of people wanting to go, but Lenny was not happy. She loved the cooking part but not planning the bus logistics for each excursion, so I took the travel aspect of our classes over completely. Thus started my life-long association with buses. I had found my niche, and I was in hog heaven.

From there I started planning trips for other groups. I never wanted payment for planning. I just liked doing it. I planned trips for my church, boys and girls clubs, a quartet that I sang with for 20 years, and anyone who wanted a trip planned.

I had plans for different groups all over the house. Finally, my husband said, "I can't live like this. Either go into or get out of business. Get all this stuff into an office or at least into one room!" He was right. I told all my friends I was going to have to stop. It did not go over well. "Please," they said. "We love your trips. Start your own business. Business is easy. All you have to do is charge." (Boy, were they wrong!)

I talked it over with Everett. He said, "It's okay with me if you want to start a business, but don't count on me. Don't ever wake me up and say, 'Can you drive? My driver's sick.' Because I won't. I don't want to know how to start a bus, let alone drive one. It would be your business and your responsibility."

"Okay," I said. "If you ever need a scrub nurse or help in your office, don't call me. I won't come. I have a company to run."

We shook on it.

To this day, he can't start or drive a bus, but he wants to buy stock. Sorry, it's not for sale. I was now officially in business, and I was scared. It was the same fear I had of not making it in nursing. I had to make it. I had to deliver what I said I could.

So, on September 8, 1980, with the family phone, the yellow pages, an old manual typewriter, and $200 I had saved from grocery money, I started my company from the kitchen table.

Chapter 2

Getting Started – Major
Issues to Address

Choosing a name became a major undertaking. I wanted to call it Bluebonnet Tours – after the official flower of the State of Texas. I went all over town looking at ready-made stationery with bluebonnets on it because I could not afford to have it made. There were none to be found. Finally, I went to a local discount store to see if they had anything I could use that was cheap. Voila! I found it—ready-made letterhead with daisies on it for $1.97. So "Daisy Tours" it was. Who would have thought a discount store would play a part in naming my company, and I had $198.03 left. I was ready to go big time.

I wanted to have a grand opening, but not in my kitchen. I would have to wait until I had enough money for an official office somewhere. I saved my money, and 3 months later I moved into our 8' x 10' office in a nearby high-rise building.

When my friend who owns a large catering business heard that I had started a tour company, he called me. He had a party ranch and was a wonderful caterer. He volunteered to do a grand opening for me – free of charge. My office was too small, but in my high-rise building, some floors were not finished out yet. He called the building management, and they agreed to let us have a "Hard Hat Opening of Daisy Tours" signifying a new beginning. He created a fantastic menu. All my old friends I had done work for came. Many of the doctors came, telling my husband, "I wish my wife would start a business." Everett's response was, "We'll see." Now I knew I had to succeed. Failure was not on the table. It was not an option, and I knew it never would be. Failure was not in my vocabulary.

The third year I made $600 profit. My son-in-law is a CPA. "June," he said. "You are working too hard to only earn $600 a year. How can you make it?"

"How much would I have made if I had quit?" I asked. "That is $600 more than I would have if I had quit. I am not ready to quit."

I needed a good client base, companies that would use my services and be faithful to me, so I set out to find them. I had to do it all by phone, because mail-outs were too expensive. I would have to build relationships. I wanted them to like my service so much that they would not even think of using my competition. I started visiting schools, hotels, and organizations, and I was able to build a client base that has lasted for years. Then and now, if I lose one, I immediately find a replacement. That way I always have a good base. It gives me confidence that I can always pay my bills.

I got to know my travel seasons. The professional football season is huge. Many military reunions come in October and November. The school year is great. Spring Break can be monstrous, with trips to theme parks around the U.S. and ski trips to Colorado and New Mexico. August and September (until school really gets going) can be painfully slow. So I save, save, save for those months and offer specials and discount rates to get extra business then.

I went after customers who would be around for a long time. The Alamo Bowl™, a college football bowl game, was one of them. Everyone was bidding to get that contract. To begin with, it was brand new to San Antonio. We wanted it, not only for the annual business, but we were also trying to build a sports image. We went after it with gusto. Our plan was to bid it low so our chance of getting it was better. However, we were not in the position to give it away. We had to make a small profit. We worked hard on it, cutting expenses where we could, and to our amazement, we won the contract. My male colleagues who had bid on it said, "No woman should have this contract. That is a man's job." "Not this time," I told them. We handled the Alamo Bowl™ like pros, and our drivers loved being a part of it. From that very first year, we had the right of first refusal. We have never refused the job; so over 20 years later Alamo Bowl™ is still our customer. It is always a fun time. It makes good money, enhances our image, and introduces us to numerous teams. Nevertheless, every year I get calls from other bus companies. "Are you going to sponsor the game this year?" they ask. The answer is always the same. "Yes, but thanks for asking." "Are you ever going to decline?" they ask. "Not likely!"

The Alamo Bowl™ was a stepping-stone to other bids. One was our military contracts, and they had an interesting beginning.

San Antonio had five military bases at that time, but the busiest one was Lackland Air Force Base, which was for basic training. This meant the base put new recruits through basic training and then shipped them off for special schools. This dispersing of the troops was what interested me. I felt I didn't have a chance for a government contract. "Maybe I could learn how to apply for one," I thought. I really didn't know where to start. Then one day I went to a transportation meeting. All my competitors were there. I was sitting between two bus company owners when one leaned across in front of me and said to the other, "It is time to bid again." The other said, "We will take care of that." I knew what bid they were talking about: Lackland Air Force Base's military contract. Now I knew I had to bid. First of all, I was angry that they thought I was not smart enough to know what they were talking about. My work was cut out for me. I was determined to try to win that contract. I needed the Department of Defense (DoD) approval. So I applied.

I went to work on it. I called some military friends for help. I got books on how to bid a military contract. I studied the route, the fuel needed, and the DoD regulations. I did my best to put the bid together correctly, and I had two military friends check it for me. Best of all, I gave them a fair price. Then I delivered it to Lackland AFB.

Six days later, I got a call saying Daisy Tours won the contract. I couldn't believe it! I got it! I would be moving military troops from Lackland AFB to Sheppard AFB in Wichita Falls, Texas. The military let me choose the day I wanted to do it. I chose Monday, as it is usually a down day for bus companies. Not for me. Not anymore. Every Monday I had 5 to 8 coaches going to Sheppard AFB. We had the contract for the next 20 years. We missed one year, but we got it back and still have it to this day. On a military bid, you just need to know exactly what information they want and how they want the forms completed. When you figure that out, it is pretty easy to bid. Was it satisfying to win the contract? Very! Was it a surprise to some big-time operations? Definitely. Was it profitable? Yes, for many years, and still is. I remember an Uncle Sam poster during WWII. It said, "Shhh. You don't know who's listening!" They were right.

Daisy Tours has a knack for winning huge contracts that come back year after year, like college basketball tournaments. After doing the Alamo Bowl™, we had experience, and that added a lot to our bid. We had a reputation for doing great work with sports teams. We were on time, every time. We had professional drivers in uniforms and sparkling clean coaches in good repair. Everything worked: microphone, lights, bathrooms, etc. In addition, I had a super staff that took care of every last detail.

The result was that we won the transportation contract for college basketball's marquis championship held in San Antonio. Our experience with sports teams also won us contracts with professional baseball teams, hockey teams, and basketball teams. All these teams were part of our base. We work hard to keep them. Because I love sports, the work is easy.

In the 1980s, buses came under the jurisdiction of the Railroad Commission, and we were required to register our name with the State of Texas. Buses are very different from trains, but that was the law and we had to deal with it. Filing our name was easy, but if we wanted to buy a bus, we had to get a railroad permit to do it. Getting that was a huge problem. I found you had to have letters to show a need, have a route you pulled on a regular basis, show insurance to cover any problems ($5 million), and be inspected by the Department of Transportation (DOT). In addition, my competitors could protest my application, if they so desired.

The other bus companies had gotten their railroad permits by having their lawyers represent them. I certainly didn't have the $30,000 to $40,000 it required to have a lawyer handle it for me. I was leasing buses from other companies, and that kept me going, but I longed to own my own coaches. I didn't know what to do. I wrote to the Railroad Commission and asked for information on what exactly I needed to do. They sent me a letter saying to fill out their application, and I would hear from them. The application cost $25. I sent in the $25 with the application filled out.

Three weeks later, I got a reply. I had a court date for a hearing in Austin, Texas, with the Railroad Commission. I had no lawyer, no regular routes mapped out, no letters of recommendation showing a need, and certainly no knowledge of how the hearing would go. Naively, I thought they were going to tell me how I could accomplish these requirements. I quickly made phone calls to friends and customers requesting a letter showing need. I was able to get six letters back. A close friend, Franklin Roe, who was a driver for a company that I was leasing from, agreed to go with me. In addition, I got my daughter, Kim, to go just in case I missed some of their instructions.

When we arrived in Austin at the Railroad Commission, I found my name on the docket. I was terrified. Since I had no lawyer, I was going to have to wing it. The commissioner that day was a lady. "That's lucky," I thought. I approached the bench and asked her if I could go last. "No problem," she said, as she crossed off my name and put me last. I waited in the court with the other applicants. Fortunately, we had brought a yellow tablet and several pencils to take notes. If I was going to wing it, I was going to listen to what the five lawyers ahead of me had to say first.

As the meeting started, it was announced that two bus companies were protesting the application of Daisy Tours on the agenda. They were informed that the fee to file a protest was $1,200 each. They considered it and then dropped their protest. I was still in the game. I was shaking so badly that I could hardly write. One by one, the lawyers came up and pleaded their case for the bus company that they represented. Franklin, Kim, and I listened carefully and took notes, recording the words these lawyers said.

"My client wants to operate between (the city of origin) and all parts in the United States and return." Quickly we wrote putting San Antonio in its proper place. "Our route will operate between San Antonio and Jourdanton, Texas, once a week on Wednesday, returning the same day."

"We have six letters of need and recommendation." We wrote what we would say, all three of us helping to get the wording just right. After listening to all five lawyers, we finally had it all down on our tablet.

Then, they called my name. "June Bratcher representing Daisy Tours of San Antonio, Texas."

I approached the bench shaking so hard the tablet was hard to read. "Your Honor, Daisy Tours wishes to operate from San Antonio to all points in the United States and return. I have six letters of recommendations and numerous signatures. The route is between San Antonio and Jourdanton, Texas. It will operate every Wednesday leaving from the Alamo at 10 a.m. and returning by 2 p.m. I will have two coaches that are DOT approved, and I humbly request a railroad permit to operate and give transportation service to the rural communities."

It was over. I had given it my best. I waited for her response, holding my breath, afraid to breathe for what seemed like forever. She studied my application. She asked me no questions. "That is bad," I thought. "I am not going to get it." Then abruptly she picked up her gavel. She pounded it on the block and announced, "Granted." I fought back tears. I had not made a fool of myself in front of all these people. I thanked her and walked slowly back to Kim and Franklin. We proceeded out the door. It was then the tears came streaming down my face. We had done it. We decided to blow $1.25 on pizza to celebrate. What others had paid lawyers $30-40,000 for, we got for just $25. From that day on, I decided that all our bus numbers would start with 25 to remind us of our humble beginnings, and that all things are possible.

We drove the Jourdanton route for 4-½ years. We never had a paying customer. One time our driver picked up a hitchhiker just for company. Then the law changed. The Railroad Commission no longer had jurisdiction, and we were free. Nevertheless, we had obeyed the letter of the law. This experience gave us our motto, "We can do that." I tell my staff, "There is a solution to every problem we have. We just have to find it." Then I ask, "Who will be our hero today and come up with a solution to this problem?" It has worked over and over again. Everyone wants to be a hero.

Chapter 3

Employees Can Make or Break You

I learned early on that drivers could make or break your company. I have a rigid training program for drivers, but they are people and things can go wrong. My driving staff can do spectacular work, but one driver can also destroy it all in one trip. They have to be on time, in uniform, dressed to the nines, smiling, assisting people on and off the coach, and be sure the coach is sparkling clean, smells good, and everything on it works. It is a tremendous responsibility.

It is also not an easy job. They have 40 to 50 lives in their hands. The coaches now are fairly complicated to operate. They have 18 computers, a 21-inch flat-screen TV, monitoring cameras, and smart tires that tell them immediately if they have a tire problem. In addition, drivers sleep irregular hours, eat when they can, and are often away from their families. It is not a dream job, but most drivers love it or they would not stick with it.

Some drivers stand out over the others. One I especially remember was Rafael. He drove our San Antonio Missions professional baseball team everywhere--I mean he did not want them to go anywhere without him. He was hooked on baseball. He begged me to let him be their official driver. His life dream was to play for a national team. His chances for that were unlikely. He was not tall and not really big and powerful. If he could drive the Missions, he could live his dream. Rafael took care of them as if he were their mother. He went to every game and most practices. Home or away, he was there. He was in baseball heaven.

The team loved Rafael, as well. Wherever they went, they always requested him to drive. All the other teams, the management, and the coaches knew him. Rafael endeared himself to everyone. When the team won the baseball minor league championship, the team members all pitched in to get him an $800 championship ring.

The next season our San Antonio Missions were sold and came under new management. The new owner had a friend at a different bus company, so Daisy Tours lost the contract. It was quite a blow. Rafael was devastated. However, we all understood the reason, and the season started without the duo – Daisy Tours and Rafael. The new contract holder called Rafael and tried to hire him away. "No," he said. "Ms. June has been good to me." At the end of the first week, I got a call from the new owner.

"Do you have a coach?" he asked. "Will you take us back?"

"Of course we will. But what happened?" I asked.

"Well," he said. "Wherever we went, everyone was asking for Rafael. They were told, 'The new manager has a friend at a competing company.'" When the news reached baseball headquarters, a directive came out. Get Rafael back immediately! He is the best driver from the best company we have ever had in the entire country. He will stay with us!"

We were back. Rafael was back. Life was beautiful again! That season the Missions won the championship again, and you guessed it. Rafael got another championship ring. Those kind of employees are like gold. They love their work and their company and we love them back.

Chapter 4

Challenges Along the Way – Including Suicide

L ate in the fall of 1980, my business was growing. My friends were supportive. The schools my children had attended offered many opportunities for business. Then suddenly disaster hit in the form of H.B. 72, No Pass No Play. The school business I had counted on was gone. I was stunned as school after school called to cancel their trips. They had to reduce their travel to one trip for the senior class only.

This was my first harsh lesson. I knew I could no longer depend on my friends and family for my business to survive. I had to diversify.

This lesson has had a long-lasting effect on me. To this day, I continually look for new areas to expand. I could not sit and wait for the phone to ring. I vowed I would never be caught again without another door to open if one closed.

I looked to two areas for help: selling airline tickets and providing destination management for conventions. After looking into each field, we made a decision. Airline ticket agencies were in great abundance, but only a handful was at the top and they controlled 80% of the sales. The other 20% trickled down to a huge number of small companies, and I would be one of them.

Convention planning had much more to offer. San Antonio had a new convention center, a convention bureau that was growing, and only a couple of convention planners in operation.

Looking back, it was a lucky move. Airline tickets were being sold online, so airlines were offering fewer and fewer commissions, while the convention industry was growing.

We added a DBA (Doing Business As) to our name because Daisy Tours didn't reflect our new service. We were now Daisy Tours and Conventions San Antonio. It was a natural fit. Buses needed conventions and conventions needed buses. It was a perfect marriage.

By 1987, we were still leasing our coaches from local bus companies, and I longed to own our own coach. My mark-up could go from 10% to 50%, but there is little you can do without money. A new bus cost about $385,000 at that time, but I could get a good used one for around $100,000. So my journey into getting a loan started. It would be a long and lonely trip.

For 7 years, I had gone from bank to bank trying to find someone to help me. Each time they told me the same thing. "We will be glad to give you a loan. We'll need your husband to come in and both of you sign for it." Everett was willing to do this. He had always been 100% supportive, but I was not willing. I just felt I should be able to get a loan in my own name. If I was going to work this hard, it was going to be for me.

Doubts began creeping in. I was making it, but just barely. Even though the National Association of Women Business Owners (NAWBO) and others had worked hard to get the Equal Credit Opportunity Act passed in 1974, I wasn't making any progress in securing a loan. Then something wonderful happened. The Air Force at Kelly Field in San Antonio offered a course to help women in business. It cost $125, which was a lot more than I could afford, but it was an opportunity and I had to try it.

The course was fantastic! It covered so many things. At the end, each of us could choose two areas that we needed more counseling in. It was part of the class. I chose finances and marketing. A financial officer came to my office twice a week. We began putting together a request for a loan. Each meeting he would give me an assignment to do before he came back. When he returned, he checked it and had me make changes here and there. After 4 weeks of counseling, I had a 37-page request for a loan.

My job now was to sell myself to a bank. They all hated to see me coming. I had been there so many times before. But, this time I had my 37 pages. I went to the bank where I had my modest account. I requested to see a loan officer.

"Has anything changed?" the clerk asked with skepticism.

"Yes," I said. "I have a loan request made out."

She took the papers. "Wait here," she said.

Soon a loan officer came out. "Who did this for you?" he asked.

"I wrote it," I replied. It was the truth. My financial officer made sure I understood every page and had made me do it myself.

"This is textbook quality," he said.

"Yes, sir. I know what I am asking."

"Have a seat. We are looking at this." Ten minutes later, he came back. "Okay," he said. "We are going to take a chance on you. We are approving $125,000."

My heart was racing. I don't know if I was happy or scared. $125,000 seemed like all the money in the world. As I look back on it, I was terrified. I was going to have to pay it all back, with interest. I had to get started. This was our window of opportunity. We got our first bus. It was beautiful to us, and it opened so many doors. There were many challenges along the way, but that first loan was our big break. Our goal was to work hard and get four used buses, then upgrade to new buses until every bus on the lot was under 5 years old. We were on our way at last.

With the $125,000, I bought one older bus. The life of a bus is about 20 years. They hold their value very well. In time, computers, TVs, Wi-Fi, and electrical outlets would change that, but back then, you could get a good used bus for that kind of money. I bought one from Kerrville Bus Company. Success was on its way. I just knew it!

Now I needed a mechanic, a couple of drivers, and people to wash the bus. The wash rack staff represent some of my most important employees. Ninety-eight percent of our business sales are by phone, so the first impression everyone has of our company is when the bus pulls up to pick them up. If the bus is not sparkling clean with everything working, we make a bad impression. So I respect these men on the rack, as they have the awesome responsibility of making our company look good. Drivers are just as important. They must have great driving skills, be on time, and help people on and off the bus. In addition, it's important that they wear their uniform. "Anytime you are driving our bus," I tell them, "you must look like you are a professional driver, not someone trying to steal the bus." My drivers have never disappointed me, including helping a passenger in need.

This story blows my mind even today. It is seldom someone tries to kill him or herself on our company property, but that is what happened.

In 2006, we put up a beautiful wrought iron fence across one side and the front of our property. The other half would be added when we could afford another $72,000. Fortunately, the two sides waiting to be finished do have high shrubbery that adds temporary protection.

Bus companies are not always in the best part of town. In fact, they are usually close to the downtown area, and ours is no different. We have a lot of street lighting, but we also have some street people around. The wrought iron fence protects our wash rack crew and drivers who come and go all night long. The main gate opens and closes by remote, so everyone feels safe.

That is why we were so surprised the morning of March 27, 2007, to find that a woman had tried to hang herself on our new beautiful wrought iron fence. It was about 8 a.m. Everyone was just arriving to work. They were greeted by a screaming woman with her head stuck in our new fence. It seemed she was trying to kill herself because her boyfriend went back to his wife.

If she really wanted to die, she did a miserable job of it. She had put her head through the fence and then dropped to her knees to break her neck. The trouble was, it was not high enough and all she did was get her head stuck between the bars.

At this point, she decided she did not want to die, and so she was screaming for help. Of course she immediately drew a crowd. Most of them were street people. They started questioning her.

"What are you doing here?"

When she explained, they all started in on her.

"You are a fool!"

"You shouldn't be seeing him anyway."

"I told you he was no good, honey."

One man was so bold that he hit her on her rump and said, "You crazy woman! You sure are stupid."

Others started hitting her backside. At this point, my son Daniel had just arrived. He put a stop to it and started trying to get her out. Her ears wouldn't let him pull her back. He tried everything slippery: hair gel, oil, water. Nothing worked. Meanwhile, she was still screaming. Daniel called 911 and asked for help.

All at once, all hell broke loose. Fire trucks and EMS arrived, along with six police cars. My staff and I stood in our doorway in awe of what was going on. When the police arrived, the crowd dispersed immediately.

"What's going on here?" a police officer asked. Daniel explained. The officer began to laugh but tried to hide his amusement. The others turned away trying not to laugh. Finally, one called his chief.

"You are not going to believe this," he told the chief, trying to control his laughter.

Daniel took charge. "Okay guys. We need to get her out." EMS attendants calmed her down. She quit screaming. That helped a lot. The police officer who called his chief came over to Daniel.

"Okay, Dan," he said. "Our chief said only the Jaws of Life are going to get her out."

Now "Dan" was Daniel, the owner of that new fence.

"No way," he declared. "Not on my new $72,000 fence. There has to be another way! I will have to clear this with our CEO, and she is not going to like this!" Dan told them.

Daniel came inside to see what we thought. How much damage will it do? Who is going to pay for it? He went back outside, but the Jaws of Life had already arrived. So had our staff and some drivers. All of them were protesting loudly.

A supervisor assured all of us that the fence could be put back in its original condition, paint and all. The police agreed and explained that it was the only option. They applied the Jaws of Life, and slowly we watched as our expensive protection bent out of shape. There was a big gap, big enough to get her head out. She pulled herself out. Free at last.

Now we had to deal with the bent fence. When EMS said the woman was okay, a firefighter came forward to repair the fence. We watched, hoping to see that he could restore our fence to its original beauty. They applied the Jaws of Life in reverse this time, and we watched as the bars slowly bent back to their original shape. You could not tell it had been part of an attempted suicide. We cheered!

We had a few choice words for the woman with hair gel all over her head proclaiming how sorry she was to have caused all this. We all learned a good lesson that day. You cannot kill yourself by sticking your head through a wrought iron fence and falling 2 feet to your knees onto the pavement – EVER!

Chapter 5

Choosing the Right Drivers — Who Is Good, Who Is Great?

There are employees you love and never want to leave, and there are those you want to forget. There are two, a man and a woman, who I want to forget. I'll tell you both stories. I was thrilled to get the young man, who would be our dispatcher, give quotes, sell the trips, represent us at bid meetings, as well as do payroll and collections. He had a nice, friendly personality and seemed very bright. He did well. He learned quickly and proved to be quite a salesman. He got to know community leaders, people in the industry, and especially those in the sports world. He was happy to be where he was, and we were thrilled to have him. I trusted him with everything we did.

After several years, we noticed a problem. Records of trips taken were coming up missing. At first, we thought they were just lost. I had all the employees looking for them. I was puzzled. Could there be something going on that I was not aware of?

Then one day my secretary came to me and said, "Everyone in this office is upset by all the records that are missing, except the one who handles the money." I was stunned. I began to watch him. He was nonchalant about it. "They are just lost. You'll find them sooner or later," he said.

Still, I could not figure it out. I called my then son-in-law, David, who has a degree in computer science. I asked him if he could check our computer for something that might give us a clue. He had a better idea. "Let's tap the phone," he said. "You can't use it in court, but you'll have a lot better chance of finding something."

That night when everyone was gone, he set up the phone tap system and put it in a locked closet. No one knew of our plan, except David and me. The next evening, we returned to listen to the recordings. I was stunned. It was my dispatcher. I had treated him like one of my own children, and he was stealing from me. It was hard to believe. I would have trusted him with my life. There were tears of regret. Tears for why he felt he had to do it.

His system was clear. He would sell a trip. Then he would tell them to bring cash to pay at the departure point. He would be there to give them a receipt. He would tell me he was seeing a bus off, which we often did just to be sure everything was going as planned. It was a normal thing to do. I decided to watch him.

The next day he met the coach, got the cash, and put it in his pocket. I was close by out of sight and saw it all happen. When he returned to the office, he posted the cash on the ledger. However, when the driver had been paid, all records of the trip disappeared. He turned in no money. This took at least a week, so I had to observe until payday came and went. It was shocking. Every minute of watching him broke my heart. I could not believe it.

Another employee and I arranged to get pictures and watch him on his next hit. It came very soon. We arrived early at the pick-up point. We filmed him arriving, giving the receipt, and getting the money. We were back at the office before he was.

We watched to see what he would do with the money. He recorded it. The next day he paid the driver, and that afternoon the record went to his car. No cash appeared.

Finally, I had enough evidence to confront him and we set it up. I called him into the office. "I'm onto you," I told him. "I know everything. How you set it up. How you called it and how you destroy the records." I was surprised how calm I was. The respect and love I had had for him was gone. He was no longer a loved employee. He was a thief.

He turned red and started to sweat. He seemed short of breath. Finally, he reached in his pocket for a roll of bills. "You got me," he said as he laid the cash on the desk. "You can have all this." "No," I said. "You keep it. I will see you in court." It was then he began to talk.

"I don't want anyone to know about this," he said.

"That's going to be impossible," I replied.

He became furious. "Just say I got fired," he said. "I trusted you," I told him. "I paid you well. I treated you like family. You have broken my heart. How could you do this?" I asked.

"I got in with the wrong crowd," he told me. "I didn't have money for the lifestyle they had. I liked their lifestyle of booze and drugs. I wanted to be like them," he rambled on. By now, he was begging me not to tell anyone. "I'll repay every penny," he said.

I told him, "Clean out your desk and leave."

The staff had heard it all. They were quiet, huddled together by my office. It was as if a close friend had died. There were tears, not for him, but for us. He left a big hole in our lives. I never pressed charges. The theft was in the thousands of dollars. We never actually put a pencil to it, and he never repaid a penny. Nine years later, he resurfaced again. He was thinking of starting his own business and asked if we would lease buses from him if we needed extras? "No thanks. Once is enough."

Other friends in the industry called to tell me he was saying he made Daisy Tours what it is today. They laughed. They all knew. News travels fast between drivers. I still have that incriminating phone tap. It's just a reminder to be careful whom I trust.

We had one female driver we hope we never hear from again. We will call her "Mary" to protect her identity. Mary's husband was a driver for another company. It was a good company, and he was a good and respected driver. Mary's husband came to me one day wanting to know if I would hire his wife. She was also a driver, but she was out of work. He told me he was not getting a lot of work. They had two children, and she needed to find a job. Mary had a good driving record.

I wanted to help, but there were no openings at that time. The only thing I could offer her was late at night meeting new recruits at the airport and delivering them to Lackland Air Force Base. No drivers really wanted the work, although it paid $40 for 1-½ hours of work. There was also a move at 4 a.m. to take troops from the airport hotel to the Fort Sam Army Post. It was a short, in town, one-way move. If she did both, she could earn $90 a day. Her days would be free to care for her children. She jumped at it and was thrilled for the opportunity.

Mary passed all our pre-employment checks and started the next week. Her husband helped her for a few days to get used to the routine. Things went well for about 5 months, long enough to meet her 90-day trial period.

It was then I started having trouble with her. Drivers started coming in and asking that they not be given assignments with her. No one wanted to say why. At first, I didn't think too much about it. Finally, a driver who had worked for me for 12 years called me at home.

"June," he said. "Our new lady driver could get us and our company in a lot of trouble. She is waiting for drivers to come in and putting us in very difficult situations." I was stunned. "What are you talking about?" I asked.

"You need to call last night's drivers in and hear their stories."

I did so immediately, with no idea what to expect. They were all reluctant to talk about it. "Okay," I said. "I can't help if I don't know what is going on."

One driver spoke up. "I'll tell you this," he said. "Her behavior was inappropriate. We are all married, and we don't want any trouble."

Finally, I was getting the message. "Okay," I said. "I am going to give each of you a piece of paper. Go into the conference room and write up your experience. You don't need to sign it. When you are finished, place the paper on the table and leave. When you are all gone, I will get them." They were in the conference room for about 15 minutes. Then they were gone.

I collected the papers, closed my office door, and began to read. I couldn't believe what I was reading. Mary was coming to work in a see-through blouse under her uniform shirt and wearing no undergarments. When she knew the supervisors were gone, she would take off her uniform shirt, telling any driver who came in, "June would die if she saw me doing this."

There was more—hugging the drivers and egging them on. The details were too disturbing to mention. I acted quickly, calling her in and confronting her with the evidence the drivers had written. I told her this was unacceptable behavior and let her go. We have zero tolerance for sexual harassment and ethnic slurs. She screamed and cried. She swept everything off my desk in one big swoop and stormed out.

Two days later, I got a call from Labor Relations. Mary had accused me of sexual harassment and said I was paying her less than the other drivers for performing the same services. They said the Equal Employment Opportunity Commission (EEOC) would be in my office the next week, and I should pull the last

2 years of payroll records as well as driving assignments for the past 2 years. My nightmare had just begun.

I contacted the attorney that I kept on retainer. "Do you know how serious this is?" he asked. "You could lose your company." The lawyer then suggested I meet with a panel of attorneys from his group to determine how to proceed. I agreed. The meeting was set up for the next morning. It lasted 5 hours, and their bill was a great deal more than I expected. They advised that I was in big trouble and that I should get a lawyer who specializes in sexual harassment charges. They gave me the name of a lawyer in Houston. Their final statement was, "The new attorney could cost you $80,000 to $100,000, and even then, you could lose your company."

I called the Houston attorney and he came at once. He interviewed my office staff and the drivers who had written the charges. He told us, "Talk to no one. Let me do all the talking and refer anyone with questions to me."

My own lawyer wanted to stay informed, but every time I updated him, I got a bill. Therefore, I canceled his services and went solely with my specialist. It seemed to me that Mary had all the rights and I had none. All she had to do was accuse me. It was up to me to prove her wrong and defend myself. It cost her absolutely nothing. I had to pay all costs. I released all the documents the EEOC wanted, and I don't mind telling you, I was scared.

Three agonizing months later, all the checking and interviewing were finished and then a hearing was scheduled. On the appointed day, Mary said she wanted a private hearing. My heart pounded when my specialist told EEOC, "There will be no hearing unless Mrs. Bratcher is present to hear her accuser."

At first my attitude was, "Please give them what they want. I will wait outside. I just want this to be over."

"No," he whispered to me. "We are not letting her off that easy. You have rights, too."

At last, I felt someone was on my side. I was shocked when the EEOC examiner agreed that I had a right to be present. Then he announced that he would interview Mary first in my presence and then let her leave.

It was hard to be quiet as lies poured out of her mouth. I wanted to cry and tell them she was lying, but I didn't. I needed to be tough and stare down her lies. Finally, she left.

Then it was the drivers' turn. They were nervous. They had to say things that were embarrassing, and they didn't want to say these things in front of me. My lawyer asked permission to address them.

"Mrs. Bratcher knows what happened," he said. "Do not be afraid to tell the truth. She is your boss, and she is being accused of very serious things. You owe it to her to tell the truth, no matter how painful that is. She is also a registered nurse. Believe me; you cannot say anything that will shock her. It will not affect your job. She does not want you to lie. She wants only the truth, whatever that is, as you see it. You are not the one being accused. You are a witness. The only thing you owe Mrs. Bratcher is to tell the truth, no matter how sordid it is." He then sat down.

The next 2-½ hours were misery for my drivers. They told it like it was, just what went on. When pressed, they gave the ugly sordid details. Then they were told they could go. As they left, one of them put his hand on my shoulder. "I'm sorry," he whispered." "It's okay," I told him. "Don't worry. It is our problem," I told them. "It will stay right here."

The EEOC presented its payroll and written work findings report to the judge. I did not get to look at them.

Four-and-a-half hours after we started, the judge told me we were finished. He would put his findings together and present it to a panel where a decision would be made. I would hear from him in 7 to 10 days.

The hearing was over, but the hardest job was ahead. There were sleepless nights and soul searching as I tried to recall every aspect of the hearing. How did it seem to go? Were there things in my favor? Was there more I could have done or said? The days dragged by. Each day seemed longer than the last. I stayed by the phone and waited each day for the mail. What would I do if they gave her my company? What if she got the company and a million-dollar settlement? There is no way I could pay it. My lawyer told me it could go either way. It just depended on who believes what.

Eight days later the call came. The judge would be in my office at 2 p.m. that afternoon. I called my lawyer in Houston. He said, "I'm on my way, June. I'll be there in 3 hours, and June, if we lose, we are going to appeal." Somehow, that was not comforting.

He arrived about 1:30. I was sick to my stomach. I kept fighting back tears. The judge arrived right on time. He was alone. My attorney and I went with him into our conference room. My staff was waiting, huddled together, in my office.

"Well, Mrs. Bratcher, I presented your case to the panel of judges," he said slowly. He seemed to be weighing each word. I wanted him to yell it out "GUILTY" or "NOT GUILTY," but he took his time as he pulled all the papers out of his briefcase.

"We find Daisy Tours innocent of all charges." I tried really hard not to cry, but the tears came anyway. My attorney hugged me and gave me a tissue. I thanked the judge.

"The panel was 100% for you," he said. "I am sorry you had to go through all this. All charges, including pay and work assignments, are dropped." He shook my hand, then my attorney's, and walked out. We rushed to my office. "INNOCENT," I shouted! "Innocent of all charges." The room erupted into laughing and hugging. They wanted to know every detail. "We are going to celebrate," they said. "Let's get some champagne!"

"Innocent on all counts" was the verdict, but there was a price to pay. It cost me over $11,000 to protect myself and enough tears and worry to last a lifetime.

I read the judge's report over and over again. Several things were in my favor, and one issue was gigantic. All of my employees had attended a class on no tolerance of sexual harassment and had signed off that they understood our no tolerance policy. This included Mary. The report said that that class had been my best defense. If you have a record that all of your employees have had a zero tolerance class on sexual harassment and they have signed that they agree to adhere to it, it is a huge indication that you are most likely innocent because you have addressed the issue with all your employees.

So how does an individual protect himself or herself?

1. Have a class taught by a qualified instructor for all employees.
2. Keep good records of payroll, assignments, and any incidents that might be harassment or ethnic slurs and what you did about them.
3. Alert your employees to report offenses.
4. Follow up in writing any employees' reports.
5. Enforce a dress code, and watch for violations.
6. Watch, listen, and be alert.
7. If you don't have a sexual harassment policy, get one now!

This is a serious matter. The more employees you have, the greater the chances of violations.

It seems impossible to me that one person, who was totally guilty herself, could cause me the grief and expense that she did. For her, it did not cost one penny.

So what happened to her? Sadly, she went to work for another bus company. They called me, but all I could tell them was that she worked for Daisy Tours and that she was not eligible for rehire.

The Federal government is looking at this sexual harassment issue and may get involved. If they do, it will open the door for a $3,000 fine just for not having a policy, plus more for punitive damages. However, if you have a policy that all employees have signed that they agree to comply with and they have had the class, it may close the door on punitive damages and only the perpetrator is charged.

If you find that a potential employee is not eligible for rehire by his last employer, think twice. Lastly, a footnote: appreciate your employees who feel comfortable talking to you about issues facing your company. Tell them thank you in every way possible and you too will survive. Even if they are driving you crazy!

It seems the longer a driver has been with us the more we have to watch for 100% compliance to DoD and DOT regulations. We had two drivers who violated compliance on a military move.

When we drop off troops at their new base, we come home empty. However, drivers are not permitted to drive more than a certain number of hours without a break to sleep. Most of the time, drivers are out of hours on the way home and need to stop at a designated hotel for 8 hours and get their rest. The hotel is paid for and waiting on them. All they have to do is stop.

Because they were empty, two drivers thought they could slip home and no one would know. I am sure their motives were not bad. They just wanted to get home. However, their plans did not go well when our dispatcher called the hotel to give one of them an assignment for the next evening, and neither of them was in the room. He had the hotel clerk check the rooms. They had gone to the front desk and registered, but they never went to their rooms. They walked out and got in their coaches and left.

We waited for their arrival at the garage, and we saw them coming in early. Too early. We said nothing to them then. We wanted to see how they logged their time.

The next day they came in to turn in their log, and we were waiting for them. We directed them to the conference room. My safety director was waiting for them. He looked at their log. It showed they had stopped and got 8 hours of rest. He then told them we knew what they had done and who had witnessed their arrival home. We also showed them photographs.

They were in big trouble. They had not only violated DOT regulations, but they had also falsified their logs. If they had been stopped, Daisy Tours would also be fined a large amount. The men apologized and said that they needed their jobs. They had worked for us for many years but had made a mistake in judgment. The penalty had to fit the crime. They were put on probation with no out-of-town trips and no military moves for 3 months.

This really hurt the drivers because the military moves were on Monday, and that is usually a down day for bus companies. In addition, the military runs pay very well. We checked their logs each day, as well as their behavior and compliance to all regulations.

One of the drivers took it like a man. He said it was a stupid thing to do and he was sorry. His behavior after this incident was exemplary. The other driver did not handle it as well. He showed no remorse. He pouted and gave us the silent treatment. We asked if he would like to resign. He did not want that. After that, he got the message. DOT and DoD regulation violations will not be tolerated, and a second violation means dismissal. We are talking safety, and we are serious.

If DOT and DoD regulations are not carried out to the letter of the law, there will be consequences. They always need to be addressed. If they are not, they will be repeated. We find the punishment is most effective when it affects employees' wallets or their assignments. Safety is our major concern. They only get one chance to make it right.

Chapter 6

Our Brush with Criminals

It was 1995 on a cool August evening. My partner, Franklin, and I had just finished a large party at a famous Mexican restaurant in downtown San Antonio. It was close to 10 p.m., and we had come in the same car so I would not have to drive home alone.

Franklin stopped at an icehouse to get a newspaper. I had the overhead light on in the car talking to Margaret Gharib, our tour director, about the following day's events. We proceeded to Franklin's house a short distance away to drop him off. From there, I would drive home and be there in 5 minutes. I called my husband to tell him I would be home shortly.

As we drove up Franklin's street, he mentioned there was a car behind us with its headlights turned off. Franklin had been a police officer for many years, and it seemed he was always suspicious of what was going on around him.

"When I stop," he said, "move quickly. Scoot across the seat and get out of here as fast as you can." I looked out the window as he turned into his driveway.

"They are slowing down," I told him. "It looks like they are going to stop."

"Hurry," he said. As he got out, I slipped behind the wheel. What happened next happened so fast, I hardly knew what was happening.

Two men jumped out of the car. A third man remained behind the wheel. They both had guns. They threw Franklin to the ground and pulled me out of the car, pinning me to the side of the car.

"We need your billfolds," they were shouting. One jumped on Franklin and put a gun to his head. The other put a gun over my heart and was yelling, "Don't move! Don't move!"

"Give them your billfold." Franklin called to me.

"He doesn't want me to move," I replied.

"Okay," said the robber. "Get your billfold, but move very slowly." He took my keys and threw them into the yard.

I leaned into the car to reach for my purse. I knocked my new designer sunglasses to the floor, grabbed my purse, and gave it to him. By now, the other man was tearing Franklin's billfold apart, throwing paper in all directions, but keeping the cash.

As suddenly as they came, they were back in their car and headed west. Franklin was up quickly.

"Hide," he said. "They don't know it is a dead-end street. They will be back." I ducked in the car and crouched down Luckily, when I closed the door, the overhead light went off.

Franklin went to the front of the car and crouched down. As they came by he called, "Stay down!" Slowly they approached the house. They saw no one, so they had no idea where we had gone. They waited for what seemed like an eternity and then drove slowly forward. Again they stopped. We waited until we could see the taillights in the distance. They went to the end of the street and turned left.

I found my phone and dialed 911 to call the police. Then I called my husband. "I'm on my way," he said. "Stay low in case they come back."

He got there before the police. He searched the yard for my keys while Franklin and I tried to piece together what had happened.

I had remained calm through the whole robbery. I remember making note of what they were wearing. They covered their license plates with towels. My robber wore glasses. His face seemed long with large eyes and he was African American. The car was a sedan. I couldn't tell the make. I was surprised how calm I was. It had happened so fast. The gun was huge and very heavy.

The calm feeling didn't last very long. As soon as I gave the police the information I had collected, I fell apart. I started shaking and couldn't stop. The tears came in buckets. I was glad we were both alive.

The police said they targeted us at the icehouse and that we were lucky to both be alive. It didn't help. I cried most of the night.

The next few days were uneventful. We heard nothing from the police. We went back to Franklin's street to see if they had thrown my purse in the bushes. We found nothing. No clues. I had hoped they had taken the money and thrown everything else away.

Two days later, there was a break. A young couple had the same experience, but with tragic results. They followed the young man to his home. When they demanded money, the young man refused and walked toward his front door. One of the robbers came up behind him and shot him in the head. He died immediately. He was 25 years old. The hunt for the robber/killers began.

It didn't take long. In just a few days, authorities identified the three thugs as the people responsible. They contacted me to confirm one of them was also the man who had robbed me. It was easy. I remember his face to this day. He was the killer.

It did not take long to get to the courts. Two of the men received life sentences, and the one convicted of murder got the death penalty.

Lawyers appealed the case through every court they could find, because the convicted killer did not want to die. He pleaded brain damage as a child from eating paint off the wall. He pleaded temporary insanity, anything he could come up with, but all appeals were unsuccessful. That was, in part, because he had confessed proudly to the police the night he was picked up that he had killed the young man. He and his friends had robbed three people after Franklin and me. Thankfully, we had given them everything we had. The defendant's attorney made one final appeal. He tried to prove that robbery was not the motive, thereby ruling out the death penalty.

The Bexar County District Attorney dismissed that claim as a last-minute legal strategy. She believed he ought to be executed.

On July 20, 2006, 11 years after the crime, he was.

Chapter 7

A Lesson in Women's Rights

The Defense Language Institute (DLI) is run by our Federal government to train international personnel to communicate in general- or special-purpose English, to assist them in learning to be English instructors, and to develop curriculum that can be used in their countries to meet their specific needs.

Daisy Tours has been fortunate to have the contract for over 20 years. One of our staff, Margaret Gharib, is their official guide, and she does all the planning and guide work for each group. Once they achieve a certain degree of proficiency, the students can go on field trips.

This is where Daisy Tours comes in. We take them on a San Antonio city tour, to Houston to visit NASA, to Fredericksburg to see a German village, or Austin to tour the State capital.

Margaret wanted to introduce them to small businesses in America and asked if they might tour Daisy Tours. We were glad to have them. Early one morning, 38 DLI students arrived with Margaret. She took them to the garage and introduced them to our master mechanic. He told them what he did and how he was regulated by the State and National DOT. He explained that his job was to keep the coaches running and in good repair. In addition, safety was a big factor. Then they met the wash rack crew and the employee who cleans and gives them the white-glove test each time before the coaches go out on a job.

From there they came inside. They saw Margaret's office and then went to dispatch where we told them how the trips were planned, how drivers are assigned, and told them about all the regulations required by the Federal Government for a business like Daisy Tours.

They got to meet two drivers, which was fun because those drivers had driven for them, and it was like old home week. Next came our Safety Department, one in-house employee taking care of logs, physicals, CPR training, fuel records, driving records, and federal inspections. The other safety officer observes our coaches on the road. He watches their lane changes, following distance, use of directional signals, and other safety practices on the road.

When the tours were over, our guests had some refreshments. Then Margaret asked if they would like to meet the owner. My office is quite large, and they all came in, some sitting and others standing.

Margaret introduced me. "This is Mrs. Bratcher. She owns the company," she said. I greeted them. Their jaws dropped. They looked at each other in amazement. I tried not to notice.

I told them how I started with $200 of grocery money, our history, and how after years of hard work, our gross sales were over $4 million (at that time). Then I asked if they had any questions. Here is where the fun began.

"Does your husband know you are doing this?" was the first question.

"Yes, he is very supportive. He is a surgeon and does not know how to start or drive a bus."

"Why does he allow you to do this?"

"I did this on my own, with his approval. He lets me have this company. I let him be a surgeon. We get along great."

"Why did he let you do this?"

"I worked 9 years as a nurse putting him through medical school, internship, and surgical training. When he got through, he had a surgical degree. I had a husband with a degree. I wanted to do something for me. He was supportive, but I didn't need his help because he was very busy as a surgeon. We agreed I would never ask him to drive or help at the office and he would never ask me to scrub in surgery for him. We shook hands on it, and to this day, it has lasted. Daisy Tours is mine, and the company makes more money now than he does."

I could see they didn't approve. I went on. "Would any of you object to your wife having a $4 million company?"

There were some yeses and some nos. One officer dared to say, "I would have to think about it."

The final question was how many employees do you have? That was the only question about the business. I was ready for that. "Fifty-seven," I said. "Five women and 52 men. I tell my staff where to go and what to do every day and they do it." "And," I added, "I pay them well."

With that, they departed. Margaret said on the way back to the base the chatter was all about how a mere woman could do all that. Later that week, on another tour, some students came to Margaret and said, "I told my wife maybe she could do something like that." Yeah, they got the message!

Chapter 8

Basic Rules of Business – Choosing a Bank

A major change came about with the tax rules. I had to choose whether to be a DMC (Destination Management Company) or in the mass transportation industry. With all those buses, I chose mass transportation, and we changed our name to Daisy Charters and Shuttles.

The year was 2005. We were in the best of times. Life was beautiful and Daisy Charters and Shuttles was at the top. We had five military contracts that generated between $20,000 and $30,000 per week, depending on how many new basic trainees were being moved. We moved troops from Lackland AFB in San Antonio, Texas, to Keesler AFB in Biloxi, Mississippi, Sheppard AFB in Wichita Falls, Texas, and Goodfellow AFB in San Angelo, Texas. All moves were on Monday and Tuesday, which are traditionally slow days for bus companies.

In the fall, on a Friday, the Air Force called and we were expecting to hear how many coaches they needed. Instead we were informed that starting the following Monday, which was 2 days later, they would book only 1, maybe 2, buses a week until further notice.

What a shock! Our contract was for 5 years and we were in year 2. The government can cancel a contract any time it wants. The reason given was that the Air Force had 29,000 recruits who wanted to join. However, the Army and Navy had not met their quota. So, they closed Air Force enrollment until further notice hoping some of the 29,000 would join the Army or Navy instead. That meant our $20,000 to $30,000 per week would drop to $2,000 to $4,000 per week.

For months, we had turned away business for Mondays and Tuesdays, saving all coaches for the military moves. Now we knew we were in trouble. We had to act fast. We were not even sure we could survive. So we got busy.

We called our entire customer base, explaining we were now available on Mondays and Tuesdays. We did the same with all other bus companies in the area who might need additional buses to help their load. Since we are DoD approved to move troops, we called all National Guard offices in Texas and the surrounding states offering our services.

We looked at our client base to see where we could expand our business quickly. We went after professional and college sports teams. We are good at that and we have maintained many professional and college sports contracts.

We let two employees go and combined sales and billing. We streamlined our expenses, cutting wherever we could. Everyone did his or her best to "bite the bullet." We survived, but we came up short of our previous year in gross sales.

So what did we learn? Primarily that the military can legally do anything it wants with a contract. The contract means nothing. It can cancel without early notice, and it does. It is our job to survive.

It was comforting to know we could survive without them, but we needed to make some changes. Here is what we did.

1. We no longer hold buses for an unsure customer.
2. If we need coaches and are sold out, we lease them from another DoD-approved company.
3. We constantly look for ways to diversify.
4. We look at trends and future developments in San Antonio.
5. We study where the economy, and especially the military, is headed.
6. We learned to treasure and appreciate all of our regular customers and give them tokens of appreciation, like a free airport transfer or a half-day city tour with no charge at Christmas.

Several of my friends in the hospitality and transportation business lost their companies after 9/11 for that very reason. You can't just maintain. You have to build constantly.

It sounds so simple, but how easy it is to be satisfied with the status quo when the status quo is good. Fortunately, a few months later, the Air Force restored our full military contract. Never again will we forsake our faithful customers to fulfill the Air Force or anyone else's possible needs, just in case they arise. I hope we can do both. If we can, it will be a bonanza for us and should result in our best year ever.

We have learned the Golden Rule. Don't believe for one minute that next year will be just like today. It won't. Good or bad, it will change. What happens next year is up to us. We have a sign in our office that reminds us of this. "So it ain't business as usual—adjust!" Never be satisfied with status quo. Never again expect success to be there tomorrow just because it is today. We are ready. If one door closes, we have another one in the wings ready to open. The following year was our best year ever!

I had a wonderful bank that over the years had loaned me $6 million for coaches. It was as much a part of our company as our drivers. They were there for me for over 20 years. The bank officer assigned to me was Ed White. I could not have asked for a better man. Every other month, my sons and I had lunch with Ed just to go over how things were going, what problems we had, and if we needed anything.

We laugh today about our fast food experience. We had just borrowed money for, among other things, four new coaches, and our bank was financing our purchases. It was time to sign off on the loan, but our office was being remodeled, and it was a mess.

Ed called. "We need to do this today," he said. "The coaches are ready to be picked up."

He came by the office. It was bedlam. "Where can we go?" he asked. I told him that my friend Katherine Shields owns a McDonald's franchise nearby and that she would love to host our loan-signing meeting. So we were off. We had a value burger, and I signed the contract for a $2.5 million loan.

It really tickled Ed. "This is a first for me," he said. "If we had purchased combo meals, we could have bought 329,489 of them with all the trimmings." Instead, I got four beautiful new coaches. Katherine understood our funny. She said, "What a loan!"

Daisy Charters and Shuttles; Ed White, banker; and Katherine Shields, McDonald's franchise owner: it was a first for all of us.

Chapter 9

Landing Major Contracts

Military contracts can be hard to land. Other companies are bidding. You have to have a perfect rating with DoD inspections, and you have to be ready to deliver what you say you can.

At one point, we had 5 military contracts requiring 11 to 16 buses each week. At each departure, we had an employee on base to supervise and be sure things ran smoothly. To keep these contracts, you have to take care of any issues that come up promptly. For instance, if an air conditioner goes out, our employee moves all coaches up one position while the problem bus goes back to the barn for repair, and another bus is sent out. This gives us a chance to take care of any problems we have before they become problems for the military.

One weekend a major problem came up. Our big move from Lackland AFB in San Antonio to Keesler AFB in Mississippi starts just after midnight on Monday morning. The government had to approve all our restaurant stops, the menus (which had specific requirements, such as having protein, starch, vegetable, fruit, and a drink), and it had to be priced within government allocations. On Saturday night, the restaurant we had reserved for breakfast notified us that they were closing and would not be able to feed the 210 troops we were moving Monday morning. This particular restaurant was large and very capable of feeding that many soldiers. We would have to find at least two restaurants to replace that one in order to feed that many people. On a Saturday night at 10 p.m., where can you find restaurants to feed 210 troops breakfast on Monday? We really had a major problem.

We got on the Internet and then the phone. Most of the calls had to be delayed until Sunday morning. About 11 a.m. on Sunday, we found two restaurants and got the meals set up. We were on a budget, so we had to get a military rate that was within their price.

You have to think of everything. Next on our list was parking our five buses. Could each restaurant park big coaches at their location? Yes! We worked it out. We were going to have to stagger their arrival unless they could get more wait staff in. They couldn't. We arranged to stagger their arrival. So far, so good. We were sweating it out. Time was not on our side. It was Sunday afternoon.

It was late when it looked like we were ready. We had 7 hours until midnight, our pick-up time. We had signed a contract to move 210 troops to Keesler AFB with two meals en route. As owner, it was my job to break the news of the changes to the base commander. We needed his approval.

I called the base and asked for the base commander.

"This has to be an emergency," they said.

"It is, sir," I replied. They said he would call me back. I hung up and waited. It was not long. I explained what had happened, that we had faxed him all the information, and that we were waiting for his approval or for any changes he wished to make.

"Wait while I check it out," he told me.

"Yes, sir." At this point, I could hardly breathe. Shortly, he returned.

"I will alert our military personnel on base," he said. "Would you please be there to personally see that everyone understands the changes and that all goes well?"

"I'll be there, sir, and thank you."

I could not even try to sleep. We had to pull this off. If the restaurants delivered, I knew my drivers would, but I didn't know the restaurants. I had never set foot in either of them. I hoped they were not "greasy spoons."

All went well at the base, but it was a frantic time for us. The drivers had to have directions to the new restaurants. They had to be given a staggered arrival time and be told how important it was that this went extremely well. Also, we asked them not to complain about the food. We are lucky the restaurants took us without even time to get more groceries.

Breakfast went well, but it was no military issue. Because the restaurants had such short notice, the troops were not all getting what you think of as breakfast food. The restaurants used what they had on hand. Some troops got burgers. Others got shrimp. Others got ham. The restaurant made sure everyone on a specific bus got the same meal. Now if they just don't compare notes, we will be okay. The troops had no idea we were "winging it." If nothing changed with the lunch plans and we arrived in Biloxi on time, we would be home free.

Finally, Monday afternoon they arrived at Keesler AFB on time. I got the call at 2:47 p.m. "All unloaded and accounted for." We did it. I cried tears of relief.

Late that afternoon, I got an email from the Lackland AFB commander. "On a scale of 1 to 10, Daisy Charters and Shuttles is a 17. Thank you," it said. Our problem, it turned out, was never their problem. That is the way they like it. That's the way it should be.

We are fortunate to have several military contracts. They are good customers, and we work hard to keep them happy. They are always precise and well planned to every detail. That makes it fun to work for them.

However, one day, I had a request that caused me to stop and rethink just how far I would go for them. Here is the proposal. They wanted me to move 12 drug-sensing dogs from San Antonio to a base in New Mexico in one of my new buses. "My new bus? With dogs?" I asked.

"Yes, that is what we need. They are being trained, are well behaved, and each dog has a master who would accompany it. They will stop for meals, exercise, and restroom breaks, just like real people. Of course, there is one overnight stop, which the military will arrange."

Now, I love my military, but did I love them that much to let dogs ride hundreds of miles in one of my beautiful new buses? They saw my reluctance. "Please come and meet with us," the Colonel said.

Off I went, my heart pounding. How could I politely say no? When I arrived, they were waiting for me. They had pictures and even a dog to show me how gentle, kind and sweet it was, as long as you had no drugs.

This is how it would work, they explained. The military would take all the seats out of one side of the bus. Crates would be arranged along the side. The trainer would sit in the seat opposite the crate and would be totally responsible for everything that went on with his dog. After dropping them off in New Mexico, the bus would return to San Antonio, empty. Again, the military would put the seats back and professionally clean the bus. There would be no trace of dog hair or dog odor. They assured me it would be ready to move people. Six weeks later, the reverse would happen to return the dogs to Lackland AFB.

It sounded simple, but it worried me a lot. I decided there was no way I could tell the Colonel no. I valued my military contracts.

Two days prior to the departure date, my new bus was dropped off at Lackland AFB to be made ready. We chose our driver carefully. He had to love dogs and be agreeable to driving the dogs such a long distance. The driver we chose was calm, cool, and capable, and he loved dogs. He was looking forward to it. I didn't see them off that morning. I couldn't watch, but I waited anxiously for the driver to call me at home from his overnight stop.

I will never forget his first words. "I can't believe it. These dogs are better than children are. They are clean, neat, no barking, and respond to every command from their trainer. I'll drive them anytime," he said. I didn't know it, but he was getting a lot of kidding about his driving "going to the dogs" from the other drivers. His attitude was perfect. He told them, "Not one of these dogs has asked me to make a beer stop." Both trips went like clockwork. The military was true to its word. Each time they returned the bus sparkling clean and smelling good. There was not a trace of dog hair anywhere. I took a lot of ribbing from my colleagues who said my customers "looked like dogs."

That was okay. They paid well and on time, and I kept all my military contracts. I was their hero. No one can say we failed to deliver, even if we were a little reluctant. There is a first time for everything. We got accolades for handling it so well.

When a major event was coming to San Antonio, we all knew well in advance.

Such was the case with a very famous college men's basketball tournament. All bus companies wanted to land the contract for that event—not just for the revenue it would generate, but for the recognition.

Every bus company in town was putting their best bid on paper when we got the news. They would choose two companies, and it was okay to pair up for the bid. They did not feel one company could handle this enormous undertaking the first time in San Antonio. This news came to all bus companies in the city and was shocking.

We all scrambled for bidding partners. Because I am located across the street from another major bus company, I thought we would make a perfect bid together. I put my bid on paper and proceeded across the street to see if the company was interested in pairing up with Daisy Charters and Shuttles. I asked to see the manager. The person asked what I wanted to see him about. I related my bidding partner proposal briefly.

I was shocked when the front desk employee told me that they did not plan to have a partner. They would bid it on their own. In fact, they had brought to San Antonio the man who had won the contract for the last year and hired him to do their bid for them. They were confident it was going to be theirs. Therefore, I did not need to see the manager. I heard them laugh as I headed for the door.

I left feeling embarrassed that I had come. Why, I asked myself, was I so presumptuous to think that such a big company would want to bid with me, a woman-owned bus company? Self-pity didn't last long. I still wanted to bid. "It will be a good experience for me," I told myself. I crossed the street quickly and went to my office. I closed the door to give it some thought.

I decided I would approach the newest and smallest bus company in San Antonio. I gave them a call, and they were thrilled. "We'll be in your office in 15 minutes," they said. That afternoon we put our bids side by side to come up with one bid. It was going to be perfect. Their office was at the airport and ours was downtown. It couldn't be better.

It was easy to come up with one bid, because both of us had completed our bid. We compared service and pricing, and by late afternoon, our joint bid was ready. Time was getting short, so we delivered our bid to be sure it was on time for the opening the next morning. I thought that the first company I approached would get the bid, but we were hoping they might award us an airport or hotel shuttle. They couldn't do it alone. Later, I heard that they had planned to bring buses in from all over Texas to do the job. They would use no San Antonio companies.

We waited for the judgment call. Finally, it came to all bidders in one email. Daisy Charters and Shuttles and my associate were the chosen providers. How or why, we will never know. We were elated, ecstatic, and then scared. Our first big men's basketball championship award. We had to pull it off.

We proceeded with all the arrangements necessary before the big basketball championship week. Routes were determined for airport shuttles and downtown hotel shuttles. We designed and prepared signage. We found volunteers to help us. Schedules for teams were researched, and appropriate buses and supervisors were assigned. There was a ton of work to do, but we had everything under control, from marching bands and alumni, to press and university officials attending.

It was 10 days before the basketball championship week. When I arrived at work, my secretary met me at the door.

"You need to call Mary," she said. "She called for you, and she was crying."

I immediately rushed to my phone to get Mary on the line. She was still crying. Through tears and sobs she said, "June, we have been sold."

"Sold? How could that be? To whom?" I asked.

"The one you approached to partner with," she said.

My heart sank. What happens now? Are we out and they are taking over? A million questions went through my head. "What do I do first?" I thought. Okay, call the basketball championship committee and confirm that it is true. I quickly dialed.

"Are we out?" I asked. "How is this going to work?"

Their answer was firm. "Daisy Charters and Shuttles won the contract. You will tell the new owner what to do. What you have done so far is great. Just keep it up. Keep moving forward. You are in command and you are doing it well. They will work for you."

I breathed a sigh of relief. Where do I start? I guess I need to call to see if they are ready to talk to me. In spite of the laughter I had received earlier, their total tone was changed. They were very nice, and I appreciated it. They would now be working for Daisy Charters and Shuttles. How I love justice! The shoe was on the other foot, and it fit well.

I got busy and assigned them the airport shuttle, and they got busy on it using many of Bluebonnet Tours' buses, as well as their own.

Daisy Charters and Shuttles took the teams, VIPs, press, alumni, and fans. These are the fun ones to have—the ones where you get the most exposure, including nationwide television coverage.

The whole thing went like clockwork, and the associate bus company did a great job for us, as well as our new "helper." When it was finished, there were accolades of a job well done. We had no major problems, and the college basketball coaches, band directors, alumni, press, and VIPs were satisfied. Newspapers never mention transportation for a huge event, unless something goes wrong. Then it is shouted! There was not a word about us in any paper, but we got letters, lots of them, from coaches, alumni, band directors, and even the press, on what a great job we had done.

That first big basketball championship contract led to a long relationship with the sports world. We went on to be awarded all of the remaining tournaments, two men's and two women's. We also got several other national sports contracts, and the San Antonio local Alamo Bowl™. By winning the Alamo Bowl™ contract, we won the right of first refusal, so we continue to have every single one of them, even today.

Why we won that first championship basketball contract, I will never know. However, it taught me to never give up! Never concede! To be successful, you have to keep trying. Even when you fail, you will learn something!

In our 35 years of business, we have done many conferences. Some small, some large, and some a dream come true. It was like a dream coming true when they awarded us a conference that would feature a re-enactment of the battle of Iwo Jima. Of all our great groups, this one was the most rewarding. What an opportunity to relive the WWII battle of Iwo Jima!

It was not easy. There were many challenges. The conference planners found a hill near Fredericksburg, Texas, where they would stage the battle. They would stage Japanese foxholes and gunneries there. Compared to putting it on, our job was easy. We would move all the people involved to the site. We set up an office in a hotel in Fredericksburg and worked out of there.

The battle would be open to the public to observe, and people came from far and wide just to see the historic re-enactment. They brought in tanks, trucks, and military vehicles. Soldiers arrived to play the part, including some from Japan.

At night, we would take everyone to dinner. Some who had actually been in the battle were there, and we had an opportunity to meet them and hear their stories. The army had staff on hand who had a chance to hear these stories and write them for the archives.

The day of the battle re-enactment everything went, time wise, just as it happened at Iwo Jima. Troops advanced and pushed back. Gunshots and cannons were heard everywhere, and small explosions kicked up the dust. They told the story just as it happened, and finally they planted a small flag on the top of Iwo Jima. The commander thought it was too small, so they raised a larger one, just as it was on that fateful day.

The photo of the second flag reached America before the first one of the small flag, so it ultimately became the world famous "Raising of the Flag on Iwo Jima" you see everywhere today.

Again, it was not the bus service. It was the wonderful people. The heroes of Iwo Jima made it so special. How lucky we were to be a part of it, to meet those war heroes and hear their stories. It was priceless!

Chapter 10

Memorable Clients

In the fall of 1992, a Mexican cosmetic company contacted Daisy Charters and Shuttles to handle their national conference. I had never heard of the company, let alone how to plan a conference for them.

After doing some checking, I found they were equivalent to a large, international American cosmetic company. I thought, "I can do that." So I gave them a call. They would all be coming from Mexico, mostly from Monterrey.

We set up a meeting. They wanted shuttles and help with speakers, tours, and luncheons. They wanted restaurant recommendations, literally everything a conference might need.

Margaret Gharib, our tour guide, was with me when we met. As we were ready to leave, they said, "Oh, we have one more thing. These families will bring their children and we need programs for 3- to 6-year-olds, 7- to 11-year-olds, and 12-year-olds and above. Can you do that?"

"Yes," I said. "We can." Then he added the bomb.

"By the way, the children only speak Spanish."

Before I had the chance to say anything, they showed us to the door. As soon as the door closed, I looked at Margaret. She looked at me. "How are we going to do that?" I asked.

"I don't know, but we will figure it out," she said.

It was late when we got back to the office. "Let's sleep on it," Margaret said. "We'll figure something out in the morning."

When morning came, we called in all office employees for a meeting. Margaret had a great idea. "Lots of the teachers in our public schools speak Spanish. At the time of the conference, they will be on summer vacation. Do you think if we started now, we could get some teachers (we only need three, and we could pay them very well) who would design a program and then work it?"

At last, we had an idea. We started with predominantly Hispanic schools. We talked to principals to get recommendations for their best Spanish-speaking teachers.

The first three teachers we interviewed jumped at the chance. It was only 4 days. The job paid extremely well, and it would give them extra vacation money.

They each designed a program for their age group, and we presented it to the convention chairperson.

"Excellent!" she said. "Perfect!"

We got rooms assigned at the hotel and registrations with any special needs of every child. We were ready to go.

The older kids were perfect. We took them for a barge ride on the river, to the Mexican Market to shop, to the San Jose Mission to learn about mission life and how San Antonio was founded. We included the zoo and fast food burgers. They were easy and very happy.

The 7- to 11-year-olds were also easy and fun to work with. Their parents did not want them to go on tours, so we planned in-house things. We had art lessons. One day a clown came, told their fortunes, and drew their pictures. It was very fun for them.

The 3- to 6-year-olds presented a problem. The parents would bring them in, but when mama started to leave, the child would cry and mama would come back. Soon we had crying kids everywhere, so many that we could not even start our program. If the child stopped crying, the mama would leave. In a few minutes, she would come back to see if he was okay and the crying would start all over again.

At 10 a.m., we made a rule. Give us your child and leave. Crying or not. Do not come back to check. The only thing you can do is look in the window, but be careful the child does not see you.

Miraculous! The child cried a minute or two and then got involved with the toys and other kids. We had been allowing the children to run the program, and when we put a stop to it, everything went well. Finally, everything was under control, and everyone was happy.

The leader of the cosmetic company invited us to everything they did and seemed hurt if we did not show up. It was our first experience with an all-Mexican conference, and we received accolades from every division.

Our motto is, "We can do that." Then comes the question, "How are we going to do that?" There is always an answer. We just have to find it.

Every once in a while, you get a client who can afford anything he or she wants. These are fun to do, as money is no object. This client was the head of a pharmaceutical company that was entertaining the ambulatory anesthesia doctors, and he wanted the best of everything. It was an easy job to plan a special, unforgettable dinner for about 75 guests.

We chose our favorite caterer again, and our favorite site, the famous missions of San Antonio. We knew that combination would impress, and we prayed for a star-filled, moonlit night.

Dinner was in the granary of the mission. It is old, stark, and was just the atmosphere we wanted. Don Strange Catering is one of the best in the country, and he showed it all here. Tables were set up with fine linens, sparkling crystal, and china that glistened in the candlelight. Beautiful fabric covered the chairs, and huge peach bows graced the back of every chair. It looked like a birthday present.

The buses arrived at the outer gate. Padres met them in long flowing robes and escorted our guests to the courtyard where they could view the historic "hornos" (clay ovens) and the ancient well. Here they had wine and appetizers passed by wait staff in formal attire, while the Parish Priest played the church bells for all to hear.

Night was beginning to fall. Once again, the Padres escorted the guests down the pathway toward the granary. Small, clay missions provided candlelight along the path. As they entered the granary, we could hear gasps of oohs and ahhs at how beautiful it was--the old and the new. A guitarist played classical Spanish guitar music in the background. The guests were served a five-course steak dinner. It was exquisite, sparing nothing, with choices of fine Texas wines. For dessert, each table got a tray of Mexican desserts. My friend was the perfect caterer. When dinner was over, their host greeted the guests. He received a standing ovation.

But, the party was not over. Once again, the Padres appeared to escort the group back to the coaches along the candlelit pathways. This time, they exited a different door. As they went out the door, they saw a beautiful sight. The mission church looked like a painting. Floodlights illuminated the facade from the base, and the moon just to the left of the church steeple was striking. It was as if God had placed it there to give them a beautiful sight and to light their pathway.

We could hear their oohs and ahhs again. Then, more Padres stood at the church door in their flowing robes and long wooden crosses, bidding them farewell and God bless. Our client was more than thrilled. "No one can top this," he said. "It was a totally perfect evening from start to finish."

Humbly, we agreed.

It was national basketball championship time in April of 2008. Daisy Charters and Shuttles had been fortunate to win the contract for every men and women's basketball championship that had ever been in San Antonio.

There was one man we will never forget. His name was Buddy. He was the team academic adviser. He was confined to a wheelchair, so he was always the first one to be boarded on the coach and the last one to get off.

As Daniel Bratcher was preparing the lift for Buddy to get in the bus on game night, it was obvious that Buddy was troubled.

Dan asked him, "Are you okay? Do you need something?"

"I'm afraid we are going to lose," he said. "By all analysis, we are going to lose." No one says we have a chance."

"Let me tell you something," Dan replied. "We've contracted a lot of championship games, and Daisy Charters and Shuttles has always driven the champions. You will do okay tonight. It's the 'Daisy Luck.' You will see."

That night Buddy's team was behind for most of the game. At the very end, however, they hit a 3-point basket, sending the game into overtime. Daisy Luck persevered, and Buddy's team was able to snatch the victory in the last few seconds and win the national championship.

Buddy could not wait to find Daniel. He nearly jumped out of his wheelchair when he got to Daniel at his bus to hug him and give high fives! There were tears in Buddy's eyes. As Dan rolled his wheelchair up the ramp to put him on the bus, Buddy gave him one last hug.

"We will always go with Daisy Charters and Shuttles, Daniel. I guarantee it," he said.

Spring of 1996 was an exciting time for the city of San Antonio. Mayors of cities from all over the country were meeting in San Antonio for a Mayors Conference. We had to put our best foot forward. Our mayor wanted to impress the country with what a great city we have: our history, our multicultural residents, our fiestas, and our festivals. They made it very clear to us that our mayor wanted to impress everyone.

The city officials decided to award the contractor for the transportation and tours by bids from various companies. They invited thirty-two companies to bid. A panel of city officials from various departments would judge each presentation and give each group points for a percentage bid. The one with the highest percentage would be the provider. Of the 32 companies, they only invited 5 to the final bid. We were one of them. It meant we had to deliver on every aspect.

For the presentation to the panel, I would cover the part about Daisy Charters and Shuttles' history and our accomplishments and why we were worthy of being chosen. Our dispatcher, AJ Ruiz, would go next describing our coaches (ages, maintenance, etc.), our safety record, and include information about our drivers, how long they'd been driving, how assignments are given, their personal safety records, their training to assist passengers, and much more. Margaret Gharib, our ace tour guide and historian, followed him. She told how the tours were designed to appeal to the client, to teach them history, art, and the culture of our state and businesses. She would provide fascinating stories about the history of San Antonio, gearing it to how it compares to their own state. I wrapped up the presentation with how we worked, how we charged, and how we delivered everything we promise. I told them how happy we were that the Mayors Conference was coming and that we were looking forward to meeting everyone involved. Lastly, we asked them for their business. We promised we could deliver everything we had said we could, and we hoped they would honor us by choosing Daisy Charters and Shuttles. We did all of this in just the 20 minutes we were allowed.

Each department head gave us a grade. At the end of our presentation, they gave grades to the conference chair, who ranked us in a percentage of the whole. We had no idea how we had fared, with so many people judging us.

We then sat back and waited for the other presenters. I thought they were good. It was hard for me to compare them to us. I am sure I am prejudiced toward Daisy Charters and Shuttles.

A few weeks later, the letter came. It explained how they rated each company in various categories.

Experience	20 points
Experience of personnel	20 points
Responsiveness to conference needs	15 points
Cost of service	15 points
Proposals scope and methodology	15 points
Experience of subcontractors	5 points
Guides, restaurants, tours, etc.	10 points

Our percentage rate was 93.8%. We were stunned. Our closest competitor was at 84.2%. We were 9.6 percentage points ahead of everyone else. Now it was up to us. Our time to deliver!

Were we scared? We were petrified, but only at first. We got to work. We engaged the best guides, the best bus companies, and hordes of volunteers who would help make our city look its absolute best.

We came to work early. We stayed late. We checked and rechecked every last detail, and we pulled it off. Our mayor was ecstatic. He told me, "The great thing about our conference is that all attendees want to come back and bring their families."

We were so lucky to be chosen and thrilled that everything went off without a hitch. A conference like this can make or break you, and my entire staff made sure it was a job well done. Our competitors even congratulated me. All the glory went to my fantastic staff, and we used their experience to get more great conferences.

Chapter 11

Favorite Tours

In 2007, we welcomed a large group of tourists from Serbia. They wanted to see and live Texas and all it has to offer. They had a vision of what Texas was...cowboy country, out on the plains with Indians and border wars with Mexico.

If they didn't come with cowboy boots and hats, they got them as soon as they arrived. They had 11 days to see all of Texas. Of course, they wanted to start with San Antonio. They knew the history, Santa Anna, the Alamo, the Missions, the Comanches. Now they wanted to see it all.

We started early every morning, cramming in as much as possible of San Antonio's fascinating history. They loved it and could not get enough pictures.

Then they announced that they wanted to go to Fort Worth, to a famous Fort Worth dance hall and the stockyards. They wanted to see the cattle drive right through downtown. They were used to traveling in Europe and were stunned to find that Fort Worth was 5 hours away. Nevertheless, their minds were set, and we prepared to go.

They paid everything with 100-dollar bills, and they had a ton of them. They seemed to be able to afford anything they wanted. So off we went at the crack of dawn. We saw the cattle drive, cowboy museums, dance halls, and the western town before we started home. We got back to the hotel at midnight.

On the way home they said, "Okay, now we want to go to the Gulf of Mexico, Corpus Christi, and to that famous south Texas ranch!" After looking at a map, they decided they needed to see Mexico, as well. So, out came the 100-dollar bills and we were set for a 5 a.m. departure.

They waded and swam in the Gulf of Mexico. Then it was off to lunch on their way to the ranch. They bought all kinds of expensive ranch-branded hats, boots, and purses. You name it. They bought it. Then we headed for Laredo, Texas. They could not go across the border into Mexico, because they didn't have multiple entry visas. It didn't make any difference. They took pictures at the bridge and shopped the state-side souvenir shops. They learned about fajitas, tacos, mariachis, dancing señoritas, and what they enjoyed the most, tequila!

Now we had a problem. Everyone wanted bottles of tequila to take home. By now, our coach was loaded, but we had some room in the luggage compartments below. We went from liquor store to liquor store, and each time they bought out the store. There were 46 people, and I believe each one purchased 10 bottles. They had them packed for shipping at each store so they were ready for overnight shipping when we got back. They had one more, huge fiesta Mexican dinner, along with mariachis, and we were off for San Antonio.

When we got to their San Antonio hotel, we had enough tequila to open a liquor store. We went straight to the overnight shipping store to arrange for the shipping. Thankfully, neither the police nor the border patrol stopped us, as that would have led to every package being inspected!

Finally, on the last night, we went to a ranch where they could be cowboys. They could ride a horse, sit around a campfire, and sing cowboy songs with a thick accent. It was a trip of a lifetime for them! By the end of the trip, we were all like family. They said it was exactly what they had dreamed of, as they had planned their trip for years. I had more 100-dollar bills than I had ever seen in my lifetime, and I had 46 Serbians who had lived the Texas dream in style.

We became very comfortable as a tour operator as the years went by. I believe the best tour we ever did was one to San Francisco.

We flew to San Francisco with our large group. We traveled on a budget airline, so there was no food. We had our entire group in one section of the plane, and after we got airborne, we provided a taco breakfast for everyone. Our Daisy Charters and Shuttles bus was waiting for us when we arrived, and we headed for the California wine country. Our home there was a beautiful winery. It was October, and the grapes were being harvested.

We started with a class in wine tasting. How to do it. What to look for. How to recognize the wine by the shape of the bottle. We visited Spring Mountain Vineyard (where the television series Falcon Crest was filmed) and tested our wine-tasting skills.

Before leaving San Antonio, we had prepared a surprise picnic for our group. We had flatware, napkins, plates, cookies, and lunch boxes for each of our tour guests. We tied a wine glass to each prepared lunch box. The next day, as the tour group came out of the Rutherford Hill Winery, they saw this beautiful picnic set up with washtubs of wine. We had prepared it the night before.

"Look," they said. "How beautiful! Someone is having a picnic!"

"It's for you," I told them. "It is all for you."

We were overlooking the Napa Valley watching the wagons of grapes being hauled in and having a wonderful picnic lunch with lots of wine. "It doesn't get any better than this," they said.

After 3 days in the wine country, we went back to San Francisco for 3 more days. They had fun touring the fishing wharf, an early morning trip to enjoy the peace and tranquility of the redwood forest, a cruise under the Golden Gate Bridge at sunset, and a cable car ride to Chinatown for an 11-course meal at a famous Chinese restaurant. On our final night, we had a beautiful dinner over the water at the then Pier 2 on the wharf.

Now it was time to go home. Our final stop was at a famous San Francisco bakery for a supply of sour dough bread en route to the airport. It also gave us time to pick up sour dough sandwiches for lunch on our budget flight home.

It went wonderfully well for our group, but other passengers on the plane said, "What about us?"

"You have to go with Daisy Charters and Shuttles to get this kind of service," I told them.

They were ready to sign up. After our trip, I got all kinds of notes and letters. "Can we do that again?" "Where can we go next?" they asked.

There are many things important to running a business, but one of the most important was not our 4-color brochure or fancy office, but our ability to back up our service claims with our performance, always giving that extra something they did not expect. It makes them feel as if they are the most important people in the world, which they are. They are my customers, and I treasure them. They make Daisy Charters and Shuttles possible, and I love them for it.

From the very beginning, Mexico has been a very popular destination for our convention groups. Crossing the border was exciting, sometimes scary, but also fun. Our destination was always Nuevo Laredo, Mexico, a short 3½-hour drive away.

We would meet early in the morning and have a Mexican street breakfast of tacos and coffee for our totally Mexican experience. En route, the professional tour guides would tell everyone the schedule for the day, including how to get through U.S. Immigration and what shops had special prices for our guests. We also would tell them about the nice things they could find in Mexico for themselves or as gifts for friends, like a beautiful hand-carved salad bowl, silver jewelry, tablecloths, colorful dishes, and tequila or other liquor they might like. We had to keep up with the current laws that limited the amount of liquor they could bring back and explained that they would have to pay tax on the liquor when they crossed back into the U.S.

We gave the passengers maps of the market place and directions on where they would have lunch, and, most importantly, the time they should be back across the border to the U.S. Tiny, fabric serapes were pinned to their shirts so the merchants would recognize them as being with the Daisy Charters and Shuttles group and give them special prices. For some larger groups, the mayor of Nuevo Laredo arranged for mariachis to meet our group at the bridge. It was an exciting day, not only for our passengers, but also for all of us who accompanied them. We never tired of going to Mexico.

On one trip, we took four motor coaches. The clients were attending a convention in San Antonio. The day was going like clockwork. Our guides, drivers, and escorts were fantastic. At 3:15 p.m., three buses were loaded and ready to depart for San Antonio, but one bus had one passenger missing. The guide for that bus was my daughter, Kim. She went back to the bridge to look for our stray.

The plan for the coaches was that on the way home everyone would have an opportunity to show their most treasured find in Mexico. We called it our "Show and Tell" segment. This was always fun, and brought shouts of, "Oh dear! I missed that!" and "Can we go back tomorrow?"

There was enough room on three of the buses to carry the fourth bus's passengers, and we gave the passengers the option of moving to one of those buses. Some of them moved over, and the first three buses left Laredo for San Antonio. The fourth bus remained behind, holding the passengers who were unwilling to leave behind a fellow group member. They chose to wait for her, not knowing how long it would be.

Kim found our missing passenger at the American Immigration office. She was a very embarrassed lady. She was from another country, and she had a pink multiple-entry form, which she had shown to officials when she crossed over into Mexico. However, coming back, the American officials discovered that it had expired and had to be renewed. They told her to go to the American Consulate in Nuevo Laredo, Mexico, where she could get it renewed between 9:00 a.m. and 3:00 p.m. on Tuesdays and Thursdays. Because it was after 3:00 p.m. on a Friday, she would have to wait in Mexico until Tuesday to have it renewed! Kim and the lady went to the American Consulate and explained the situation, the conference in San Antonio, the bus waiting on the American side, but she got the same answer. "We will be happy to renew it between 9:00 a.m. and 3:00 p.m. next Tuesday."

"Okay," Kim said in her most firm voice. "If we have to wait until Tuesday, we will wait right here," and she and the lady sat down in chairs across from the official's desk. Immediately she was told, "You can't wait here." Kim again was firm. "We have no place to go. We will wait here." There was a flurry of whispers while all the officials went to another room. Shortly they returned with a special message. "Well, I guess we could fire up the machine and get it done now." Five minutes later, it was official. The date on the multiple-entry form was current.

Kim took the lady by the arm and quickly walked out the door. "Don't look back," she told the lady. "Just keep walking." When we get to immigration, let me handle it." The two of them hailed a cab and asked to be taken across the bridge. When they got to immigration, however, they directed them to pull over so they could examine all the papers thoroughly. They did not allow Kim to answer any questions directed to our foreign guest, who had to receive and answer all the questions in English, not her native language. Eventually, the officials allowed Kim and the lady to proceed over to the U.S. side.

Not knowing that the fourth bus had waited for them, they planned to rent a car to get back to San Antonio. Imagine their joy when they entered the U.S. and saw our Daisy Charters and Shuttles bus waiting for them, filled with loyal friends who would not leave someone behind. As they got on, everyone cheered, and the lady cried as she hugged Kim. The "Show and Tell" on this bus was special when the delayed passenger told everyone how Kim had saved her and brought her back to America.

Many people begged us to go back to Mexico the following day, but we could not work it into their schedule. By the end of the conference, everyone knew the story of the outdated multiple-entry form, and they thought Kim and Daisy Charters and Shuttles were awesome.

It was nice. We could feel the love.

Chapter 12

Tours You Never Forget

Daisy Charters and Shuttles is fortunate to work with many sports teams. Through the years we have worked for many professional basketball teams, as well as almost all of the first-level hockey teams. One time in 1989 when the Chicago Bulls were in town, we saw up close how fun and personable those men are.

My sister's son, Tommy, was 12 years old at the time and a huge sports fan. I would often hire Tommy to help load and unload luggage on the bus for different sports teams. Over time, he was the proud owner of many professional basketball team players' autographs.

Tommy loved to hang out at Champs Sporting Goods store, and although he was too young to work full time, the manager told Tommy he'd pay him $200 to paint the inventory room and the hallway in the back of the store. That day Tommy got all the painting done and was leaving quickly. The manager asked why he was in such a rush to leave. Tommy told him that his Aunt June had hired him to meet the Chicago Bulls at the airport when they came in to play against the San Antonio Spurs and to do all the transfers of their luggage and equipment to the Daisy Charters and Shuttles bus while they were here.

The latest Air Jordan basketball shoes were soon to be introduced to the public, and although they were not yet on the market, each sporting goods store had received one pair to use for promotion of the upcoming release. When the manager heard Tommy would be helping the team, he gave Tommy his one pair and said, "Tommy, I'll give you $500 if you can get these autographed."

A few months earlier, my daughter and son-in-law were on a road trip to West Virginia. In a small-town mom and pop sports store, they happened to come across a pair of the first Air Jordan shoes that ever came out. They were bright red and Tommy's size. Because it was unusual to find an original version of the shoe, they bought them for him.

So, when Tommy was helping transfer the team to the arena for the game, he took both pairs of shoes with him. Michael Jordan arrived separately from the rest of the team and was running late to the warm up. It would not have been a good time to ask for an autograph, but Horace Grant had taken a liking to Tommy and gave him a floor pass to watch the game from the sidelines.

After the game, the whole team got back on the bus. As usual, I had given Tommy permission, after he finished loading equipment, to go on the bus and see if he could get any autographs. The Bulls team all felt like they knew Tommy now, and every team member was happy to autograph the red original Air Jordan shoe as Tommy went down the bus aisle. Michael Jordan, however, was in the second-to-last row, asleep. He was sprawled across the aisle, his body on one side with his legs extending across the aisle to the seats on the other side. Tommy would not think of waking him up. However, before Tommy left, Scottie Pippen asked him to retrieve his brief case off the back seat of the bus. As Tommy was carefully stepping over Michael Jordan's legs, he woke up.

"I'm so sorry, Mr. Jordan. Mr. Pippen asked me to get his brief case."

Michael said that it was no problem at all and moved so Tommy could get the case. Now was the time.

"Mr. Jordan, would you mind autographing two shoes for me?"

"Not at all!" Michael replied.

Tommy gave him the red pair that the team had already signed for him. Michael was surprised that Tommy had an original pair and happily added his signature to the rest of the team's signatures. Then Tommy pulled out the pair that his manager had given him. Michael's face went pale.

"Where did you get these?" he asked.

Tommy explained that his manager was sent only one pair for the pre-release promotion and that if Tommy could get them signed he'd pay him $500. That explanation satisfied Michael and he gladly signed that pair also, this time with a silver pen. Then Michael Jordan took off the shoes that he was wearing, the ones he'd just finished playing in that night, and gave them to Tommy!

When the team bus reached the airport, Tommy was there to transfer equipment and luggage to their private airplane. As they were about to board, Horace Grant came rushing over to Tommy explaining that he'd left his brief case on the back seat of the bus. Would Tommy please run grab it and bring it to him? Tommy hustled to the bus, found the brief case, and brought it to the plane. The team had already boarded, and the security personnel wouldn't let Tommy take it on board. The security guard offered to take it to Mr. Grant for him. There was no way! Tommy had been given an assignment and he had to complete it himself. The security guard was getting the flight attendant's attention when Horace Grant himself leaned out the airplane door and demanded, "Let that kid up here with my stuff!" Tommy was able to go on board and ended up staying 10 minutes or so visiting with the team and getting to see the inside of the Chicago Bulls' team plane.

Before he left, Phil Jackson gave Tommy a $100 tip for such good service for the team. Horace Grant gave him $100 for retrieving his brief case. His store manager paid Tommy $200 for painting that day plus $500 for the autographed shoe. And I paid him $100 for working for me. All in all he earned $1,000 that day! Plus, he has a pair of the original Air Jordan shoes, signed by the whole team, and the pair Michael Jordan had worn during the game.

When the team got back to Chicago, there was a post-game interview on the radio. Horace Grant talked about the great Texas hospitality that he had experienced and even mentioned Tommy's name on the show.

Three weeks later, a prominent San Antonio businessman somehow heard about Tommy's autographed Air Jordan's and got his phone number. He called Tommy and offered him $15,000 for the pair of shoes. Tommy thought a lot about the offer, but in the end he decided to keep the shoes. He still has them today.

Another tour that we will absolutely never forget happened early in our company when we had an issue involving a friend who was a legislator. I had worked in his campaign and saw him re-elected to 7 terms. When I needed to move into a larger space, we found a space right next to his office in a very nice high-rise office building.

At that time, we were doing ski trips, and we had one for a group of teachers going to Colorado. When they were not able to get enough people, the teachers asked if we could help find them 2 or 3 more skiers to fill the bus. We were happy to help, as the school was a good customer. We put an ad in the paper and soon a woman called to book the last two seats.

When she came to our office to pay, we were not open yet, so she went next door to my friend's office, left her check there, and got a receipt. She wrote a check for $1,350.00, and we gave her a receipt on my friend's stationary that said, "$1,350.00 paid in full" and the date. They were happy to help.

When I got to the office, my friend came over with some news. He was smiling. Well, more than that. He was laughing out loud.

"Do you know the lady you are squiring to Colorado?" he asked.

"Yes," I said, and I explained that the teachers needed two more people.

"Well that's nice," he said. "You've got two. Do you know you have one of the local Madams going with you?" I was stunned. "Are you sure?!" I asked.

"Positive." He could barely keep a straight face.

I didn't know what to do. I was sure the teachers would have read about her. I couldn't let that happen. I called for legal advice. My legislator friend loved teasing me. In the morning, he would stick his head in the door and say, "Are you taking the Madam somewhere today?" He would do it several times a day, inquiring about her health, her schedule, or some other ridiculous question.

Finally, I got weary of it. So the next time he came in, I told him that I would like to talk to him. I pointed out that "the Madam" had a receipt on his stationary that showed $1,350.00 paid in full. It didn't mention any ski trip, so he might want to consider how that might affect him.

He went ballistic. "You've got to get that receipt!" he screamed.

That could represent several visits to the Madam, I told him. He was livid and scared. "What are we going to do?" he asked.

"Oh, it's 'we' now," I replied.

I told him I sought legal help. The lawyer advised me to call my customer and tell her the tour had closed the day before. She was supposed to have brought the money in the day before, and she knew it. That is why we closed. We assumed she was not going.

"Well, call her," he shouted! "This cannot get out. It could ruin me." I called, and she was very nice. "I was afraid of that," she said. "I knew I was late."

"Bring in your receipt," I told her, "and my staff will have cash for you." She agreed.

That afternoon she came in. I got the damaging receipt and returned her cash. The friend was watching from his office. As she left, he hurried in. He had an affidavit he wanted me to sign saying he was totally innocent. I signed it. After all, he was my friend and he was innocent.

2008 was bad for hurricanes. First, we had Dolly. She was not too bad. We just moved many people out of South Padre Island and back again. That was easy. However, Gustav was a little harder. It was a lot more worry, but we handled it.

When we showed up to help with Gustav, we knew we were in trouble. FFMA (Federal Emergency Management Agency) had called and wanted all our coaches to join the coach pool out at Kelly AFB. We declined, as we had signed contracts with three nursing homes in case of a hurricane, and we had to rescue them first. After we moved them, we would go on to children's homes all along the Gulf Coast.

A large, international oil and gas company wanted to book buses for us to pick up their employees along the Gulf Coast, but they wanted to wait and see how the storm developed before sending us down there. We held their buses for 3 days. Then I had to call them and tell them there is a point when it is too late for us to go in. Make a decision now! They waited 2 more days. It was a Friday afternoon about 4 p.m.

"Okay," they said. "We are ready."

We checked the weather report. They had waited too long. I called our contact. "I'm sorry. It is too late. We won't send our half-million-dollar coaches into hurricanes. You will have to make other arrangements."

Thankfully, they agreed. They had waited too long. About 10 p.m., we got a call. They had made it to Houston, and they would fly to San Antonio, arriving around 3 a.m. We were to be at the airport to get them. Fortunately, they were on time, and we took all 300 of the oil and gas company's officials to the historic downtown Menger Hotel.

They stayed through Saturday, but late Saturday night they called.

"We need to get to Texas City tomorrow."

The storm had done a lot of damage, and they needed to get a core group in to appraise what was left.

No roads were open. All of the FEMA officials said, "No way."

Early Sunday morning we got clearance for one coach. We would have a police escort all the way to Texas City. San Antonio police would go as far as Houston. Houston police would pick us up and take us to Texas City. FEMA officials would meet us outside the city and take us from there.

Departure time was set for 5 a.m. We arrived at the hotel at 4:45 a.m. An 8-person team was waiting. They helped us load all kinds of non-perishable food, water, sodas, and medical supplies. No families could come.

Finally, at 5:45 a.m. we departed. Police in front, lights flashing. We were off to inspect the refineries and the rigs. We made it to Houston without any problems. From there the going was rough. We had many detours. The police escort helped tremendously. We were traveling in daylight, and that helped because there was no electricity and few open roads. There was glass and debris everywhere. By the time we reached Texas City, our driver was exhausted.

After he got his 8 hours rest, we told him he could go back to San Antonio. However, there was one catch. Stranded people were being rescued from rooftops and trees and anywhere they could reach to wait for help. They needed to be moved to shelters, and we had an empty coach. We agreed to help.

A police escort took us as close to the raging water as we could get. As people were brought by helicopter or boat, they were given water, an MRE (meal ready to eat), and put on our coach. They were tired, wet, and exhausted from waiting for help to come. When we had all the seats filled, we headed back toward Houston. This time we had no police escort.

After 2 hours, we were running low on fuel. Where there was an open gas station, there were long lines of people waiting, hoping the fuel would not run out until they got to the pump and filled their tank.

Our driver called San Antonio to tell us of his problem. I called FEMA to see if they could help. He got our location and said he would call me right back. A few minutes later, he called.

"Stay on your route," he said. "At the city limits of the next town, an officer on a motorcycle will be waiting for you. Follow him. Be sure you stay with him. He will get you through traffic."

Sure enough, at the city limits, the police officer was there. He motioned for us to follow him as he turned on his flashing lights. People saw him coming, and we had a clear path.

The police officer took us right to the local electric company lot and motioned us to a gasoline pump. An attendant filled our tank, and the police officer motioned for us to, once again, follow him. With lights flashing, he easily got us to the edge of town where he waved goodbye, and we moved on.

We don't know his name and never will, nor do we even know the city whose electric company gave us the fuel. It kept us going, and at the time, that was all that mattered.

When we got to Houston, we were directed to a shelter first and then to a hospital.

The people on the bus were no problem. Most were sleeping. They were dirty, water soaked, and glad to be alive. They ate the MREs and went to sleep from exhaustion.

In our haste to help rescue, we forgot one thing. We should have covered the seats with plastic. Our seats were soaked. Mud was everywhere. The bus was in no shape to do more without a good cleaning. Our coach returned to San Antonio, but it was too dirty for our wash rack crew to clean. It had to be steam cleaned.

A lesson learned and 57 people rescued from Gustav. Who said the bus business is not challenging?

Hurricane Katrina back in 2005 was another story. The people of New Orleans were in real trouble.

Again, FEMA called. Could we help? "People are drowning. How soon can you get here and how many coaches do you have?"

"Give me an hour," I told him. "I can have 5 buses ready to go."

I called the office staff into my office. A job was given to each person.

"Gloria, you go get a lot of non-perishable food, water, and sodas. David, you go to the bank and get $500 cash for each driver. Weldon, you get the coaches ready. Be sure they are fueled. AJ, you get the drivers down here. Hurry. Lives are counting on us."

Everyone sprang into action. The rest of our staff prepared the paperwork. Channel 5 called to see if we were going. "Yes," I told them. "We will have 5 buses on the way shortly."

"Can we come and film it?" they asked.

"No, I'm sorry. You can't be in the way."

"Can we film if we are across the street?"

"Only if you stay out of the way!"

Forty-nine minutes after we got the call, our 5 buses pulled away. A film crew was across the street filming. When they came to a roadblock, police let them go through. Driving was tough. Trees were down and fences blown away. When they got to Rt.12, they left IH-10 East and went as far as they could to get to New Orleans. Somewhere along that route, police met them and took them through neighborhoods and side streets to get them as close to the water's edge as they could go.

One by one, they were loaded with survivors and told what city to go to. Some were taken to Baton Rouge, some as far as Houston or even Dallas. As soon as they dropped off their passengers, they were to return to New Orleans. Our drivers ate what Gloria had packed. Passengers ate MREs, but not the drivers. There was no place to get any rest. All DOT regulations were dropped. "Drive as long as you can," they were told.

They called in to let me know where they were. "Stop," I told them. "Get some hot food and find a place to stay. You have money!"

"June, there are no restaurants, no hotels, just devastation."

I should have known that.

One driver called. "I am loaded and going to Houston," he said. "There are 3 of us. Can you find us a room for one night? We are exhausted."

"I'll do it," I said.

I started calling hotels in Houston pleading my cause. "I'm sorry, we are full," was always the answer. Finally, I called a friend at a Houston hotel.

"Let me see what I can do for you, June."

She called back. "I have one room and one linen closet. I can put a mattress in the linen closet and the driver in there can use the bathroom in the one room."

I jumped at it. I called the drivers. "Go get the biggest steak you can find," I told them. "Then go to the hotel. I have one double room and a linen closet. Get your 8 hours and get back on the road."

They got to Houston at midnight and dropped the people at the reception area. There was one problem. No steak houses are open at midnight. The only thing they could find open was an all-night fast food restaurant and they took it. It was the best meal they had had in 4 days. When they got to the hotel, they had their first showers in 4 days! They got their 8 hours, picked up breakfast at a local fast food restaurant and hurried back to New Orleans.

Seven days after the drivers left, they returned to San Antonio tired. No, exhausted is more like it, but they felt good about what they had done.

A couple of months later, we got a nice surprise. FEMA recognized the drivers for their "contribution to saving lives."

Sometimes we feel really good about what we can do just because we own buses.

A Trip from Hell

It was summer, and I was finally getting a long-awaited vacation. I was going on a cruise through the Netherlands to see the tulips. They were absolutely beautiful, and it was the most relaxing vacation I had ever had. I was not worried about the office. My sons were there, and I knew the business was in good hands. The only major trip scheduled was three buses going cross-country from San Antonio to Virginia. We planned everything. The buses were chosen and completely checked out.

The route was established and meal stops planned. Everything was in order. I was comfortable with it. Little did I know that anything that could go wrong would.

Our experience had taught us that when things go wrong early in a trip, problems seem to follow the group throughout the tour. Our nightmare was only beginning.

Everything went well from San Antonio to Atlanta. Then things started going haywire. Bus number 2 hit a curb with the front right tire and it blew out, causing two windows above it to shatter. Two other buses stopped to help. Not only did we need to replace the tire, but also the two shattered windows. It was there that we opened the back of the bus. To our dismay, they had not pushed the oil dipstick all the way into lock position, and there was oil all over the entire engine. This bus could go no further. Fortunately, the group was staying in Atlanta that night, and the two other coaches got them to their hotel.

The call came in to San Antonio, "We have to have another bus right away." We got right on it. We dispatched a coach with two drivers to drive straight through to Atlanta. We also hired a local coach to do the city tours of Atlanta the next 2 days. That would give our drivers time to get there and get their required rest before returning to San Antonio.

It was then that we got the call. "The bus is going nowhere. It will have to be towed to Roanoke, Virginia, to be repaired." Now this was getting expensive, but that wasn't all. We had to pay the local bus company that rescued us for 2 days, the 2 drivers who delivered the replacement coach and the airfare to fly them home, and the tow company who took our damaged bus to Roanoke. Eventually we would have to fly a driver to Roanoke, Virginia, to bring our bus home. We assessed our loss and hoped it was over. We still had 8 days to go. We tried not to think of our experience of "when the first part of a trip goes wrong, it follows all the way across country." "Please God, help me get through this."

We had one more blow coming. Everything went well for several days, and we were on our way home. Finally, we thought, "Ok this is it. We are going to make it home—WRONG."

On day 2 of the return trip, our buses were going through a national park when a buzzard did a swoop on one of our coaches and went straight through the passenger side of the windshield. Fortunately, no one was hurt, but the windshield was ruined. To add to that, the frame was bent. We had the bus escorted to the closest town between our two remaining buses. We were back to square one. We had no options. We would have to hire another bus company to bring our passengers home. We located one close by, and it was there within the hour. Our driver would stay with the damaged coach to bring it home. He was there 5 days waiting on it. Our three coaches finally made it home with no more problems. You would think a group that had that many problems would be very unhappy. They were not. They thought it was an exciting trip and are still our customer today.

We found it to be the most expensive trip we had ever put together, but we had learned a great lesson. It is not the difficulties you encounter, it is how you handle them and how your drivers react. Attitude is everything, even if it is a trip you want to forget.

There are situations we find ourselves in that just happen through no fault of our own. We had one such incident. At Daisy Charters and Shuttles, we pride ourselves on never promising anything we can't deliver. It is a prime principal of business; however, this is what happened.

A client called and booked 3 days of service with us for a small conference. It was all local service and we sent him a contract. It was a very normal booking. We assigned our driver to drive all 3 days.

Shortly after he went out on the first day, he called me saying, "June, I can't do this."

"What do you mean you can't do this? What is wrong?"

"You don't understand," he said. "They are all dressed in red. Red dresses, red shoes, red hats, red earrings. Red, red everywhere." He sounded frantic.

"What does that have to do with it? Maybe they are a club. They have a signed contract with us for 3 days and they can wear anything they want."

"June," he said defiantly. "There are 32 men on my bus and they are all dressed like women." Now our driver is a macho guy, and I could tell he was hurting. "What will people think?" he said.

"You know we always deliver what we say we will. You finish the tour today and you won't have to drive them the next 2 days, I promise. And, please be pleasant. Don't judge; just do your job and deliver what we said we would."

"Okay," he said. "But at 5 p.m., I am through. I'll do it for you, Ms. Daisy, but right now I am going to hide."

I immediately checked to see which drivers were available for the next 2 days. We could move five around, and I called them in. When they arrived, I explained the situation and said I needed a volunteer or even two volunteers. I tried to be flexible but firm. There was silence.

"Who will help me?" I asked. They were having trouble trying to be serious, but I was dead serious. One by one, I called on them.

"No, Ma'am."

"I am sorry."

"I just can't."

"Are you serious?"

Finally, the oldest amongst them spoke up. "I've been driving for 38 years," he said. "Nothing shocks me. I've seen everything. I'll do it both days! Relax, you guys. Go home. I can handle this. It doesn't threaten my manhood."

So he was my hero. We delivered the service just like we said we would.

I put out a notice to all drivers. There will be no taunting or teasing, and I mean it. To do so would mean dismissal.

The service went perfectly. We completed the job in good faith. A few days later, a well-dressed man came into my office. He had a $100 tip for our first driver and $400 for our hero.

Later that year at Christmas, there was a big package under our tree. A tag said, "To our hero with love from Santa." All the drivers came in to see him open it. It was a bright red dress. Santa had been shopping at the local thrift shop. There were red shoes, red earrings, and red gloves. All my drivers were grinning broadly at their little joke, but he never cracked a smile. Then he said, "Didn't you guys get the memo? It is blue this year." He is so cool. No one can get ahead of him.

The drivers saved our reputation by delivering what we promised, and we all learned a good lesson in respect and not judging others.

I told them, "We are also being judged on our service, our coach, our attitude, and our tolerance." We needed to do the right thing, and we did. Our motto is, "We can do that!" And we did it with dignity and respect.

I thank God for a driver who delivered and drivers like him. He was my hero – again.

When you own a bus company, you worry a lot about accidents. We have a strong safety program that is enforced. Even with that, things can happen that are not your fault. That is exactly what happened to us.

We move troops from Lackland AFB to Keesler AFB in Biloxi, Mississippi. We leave very early in the morning to get there in time to check them in and be on time for dinner. Our departure time is around midnight. We load and leave heading east on IH-10 towards Houston, TX. We stop for breakfast at 2:30 a.m. in Schulenberg, Texas. Then have lunch in Denham Springs, Louisiana, from 9:30 a.m. to 10:30 a.m. We arrive at the base by 2:00 p.m. It is a tight schedule. When we leave Lackland AFB, it is still dark, but there is very little traffic on IH-10 East. Most of the traffic is large trucks that travel all night.

Early one morning, our buses had just departed. There were four going to Keesler AFB in Mississippi. Before they got 45 miles east of San Antonio, our first driver reported to the second driver that it looked like a car was about to get on the highway going the wrong way on the interstate. Bus #1 and #2 got by her with no problem. Bus #3 went to the right and was able to get out of the way. He did not have time to call Bus #4. Our driver in Bus #4 saw her coming. He could not go to the right because two 18-wheelers were trying to get off the road to the right. Our driver decided the only thing he could do was go into the median and give her the whole road. He moved to the median and stopped. At that point, she had the entire road. At the last minute as she approached, she turned her wheels and drove into the parked bus, striking the front left side with a huge impact. She was killed immediately.

After checking his passengers, our driver determined that two had minor injuries. Everyone else was okay. He dialed 911 for the police, then the Base Command Central to report the accident. They both responded immediately. One of our wounded soldiers had a scratch on his arm. The other, a woman, had one on her leg. Neither wanted to go to the hospital. They wanted to stay with their group. Military regulations required they be examined, so they were transported to nearby hospitals.

I got to the site as soon as I possibly could. Of course, two news stations were there taking pictures. The fact that the woman died looked bad for us. Meanwhile, my safety officer had sent a replacement bus. When it arrived, the police told me to move all my passengers to the new bus and leave immediately.

Later I would have to answer to the Base Commander as to why the bus continued to its destination. My answer was the truth. The police told me to go. Nothing ever came of it. Our safety officer picked up the driver of our coach and took him to our office. He would wait there with the driver until the laboratory opened and we could get a required drug test. The driver was shook up, naturally, but thankfully none of our troops were seriously hurt. At 8:00 a.m., he had his test and it was negative.

What I wanted to know was why she did it. The police could tell I was distraught. The captain came and took me aside. "Don't worry about this," he said. "Your driver did everything he could by giving her the entire road. There is more to this story than you can see right now, but here is my card. If you need me, I will go to court with you." His words were comforting, but never the less, a young woman had lost her life.

I expected the worst. A few days later, a person called and asked me to come to Lackland AFB for a hearing. They had researched it thoroughly. The young woman had just left a bar at the next exit. She and her boyfriend had been fighting, and she threatened to kill herself. Her alcohol level was very high. I can understand if she wanted to die, but why try to take innocent people with her. Later, I found out she was going 107 miles per hour when she hit our coach.

Nothing EVER came of this whole incident. I never heard from the family, the military, or the police again, but it has bothered me to this day. Now, 33 years later, thankfully we have never had a fatality. In fact, in 2013, the United Motor

Coach Association's 1,100 members named us Safety Leader of the Year.

I often wonder about the woman. Did she have children? What was her family like? Why would she do such a thing? I will never know the answer to these questions, but my heart and soul will always regret that she used our bus to end her life.

Chapter 13

Giving Back To Your Community

One experience at Daisy Charters and Shuttles is an unusual one.

We had a young man who was interning with us for a year. He was from Switzerland, and his sponsor was the Rotary International. His name was Fabio, and we learned a great deal from him. One day after returning from a Rotary meeting, he came to see me and asked if I had any positions open for a man who desperately needed work. Since Fabio didn't know any of this person's skills, he thought I should talk with him. A meeting was set up and a committee formed the interview.

It turned out the man was on a refugee program through the Rotary International and Catholic Charities. Here was the deal:

Would I hire a man who....

Knows very little English

Is a hard worker – but has no skills

Is crippled and walks with a limp

Is a refugee from Somalia, and who . . .

If he can learn English and get a job, he plans to bring his wife and eight children to America. Otherwise, he goes back to Somalia and slavery!

Wow – did they ever know who to ask! I saw Hotel Rwanda. How could I say no?

We didn't have a job for him, so we created one. No one could pronounce his real name, so we nicknamed him "Dittie." It sounded similar to his real name. He would start at $7 an hour, as an assistant to our Plant Manager.

Our plant manager is Daniel Bratcher, and he is perfect for the job. He is patient, kind, soft spoken, and a good teacher (and Aggie). Daniel is in charge of drivers, mechanics, AC, bodywork, wash rack, the property, and the buses. He could use some help. I assigned Daniel to Dittie.

I didn't know the magnitude of what I had asked Daniel to do. Dittie had some problems. He was tall and slim with the weight of the world on his shoulders. He had been beaten and tortured. He was very bright and had many good qualities.

One day we had a client from Italy looking at our coaches. He only spoke Italian, and we were trying to communicate using Spanish, which is similar to Italian. Dittie was close by washing a bus. When he saw the trouble Dan was having, he came to Dan and said, "The man wants to know how many seats are on the bus."

Daniel was stunned. "Dittie," he said. "Do you speak Italian?"

"Yes, Dan Boss."

Dittie interpreted for him. Later, Dan asked him if he spoke any other language.

"Yes, Dan Boss. Somali, Italian, French, and I am learning English."

"That's wonderful," Dan told him. "Where did you learn Italian?"

"I don't want to talk about it," Dittie said.

"Okay," Dan replied, and they never spoke of it again.

Daniel started at ground zero with Dittie because he is still suffering from his past. For instance, you have to be very careful to mean exactly what you say. When Daniel said, "Dittie, run to bus 2500 and get the mileage book," Dittie ran as fast as he could. He came back breathless.

Dan said, "Dittie, you don't have to run to the bus. You can walk."

Dittie said, "No, Dan Boss. You said run." Dan explained that we say run to the bus, run to the mailbox, but we mean walk. "Then why do you say run, Dan Boss?"

"Dittie, if I want you to run, I would say run fast."

"Okay."

One day we celebrated a birthday in our front office. We all went out for breakfast. Dittie was invited but didn't want to go.

"I don't know how to do it," he told Dan. It meant he didn't know what to do at a restaurant or how to act.

Dan told him, "You just do what I do, Dittie. You will have a good time."

Reluctantly, he went. The server gave him a menu. Of course, he couldn't read it. He looked at the pictures and pointed out to Dan what he wanted. Dan told the server what his friend wanted.

They brought our breakfast. Dittie got a big pancake with a whipped cream smile, a cherry nose, and chocolate chip eyes. He had ordered from the children's menu. No one laughed. Dittie loved it, and he was pleased with his first meal at a restaurant. We all enjoyed that.

That afternoon we sang to Cindy and had a cake. She blew out the candles and opened her gifts. Dittie and Dan were there.

On the way to the garage, Dittie asked Dan, "What is a birthday?"

Dan explained, "It is the day you were born, Dittie. Cindy was born this day. We celebrate her life. What day were you born, Dittie?"

Dittie answered, "I don't know. It was a Monday or Friday."

Dan said, "Well, let me see your passport." It said January 1, 1954.

"No, Dan Boss. Everybody in my group from Somali got January 1. Then they look at my teeth and my bones and tell me 1954."

Dittie had no birthday. No special day. So we decided to give him one. We went back to a 1954 calendar. March 18, 1954, was a Monday. When March 18 came, we surprised Dittie with a birthday party. We went out for breakfast. We had a cake and candles and gave him a beautiful leather western belt. We also gave him a card for his billfold. It said, "Date of birth, March 18, 1954."

After we sang Happy Birthday and he blew out his candles, Dittie and Daniel were going back to their office. Dittie said, "Dan Boss, I really like that cake part."

A few weeks later, we had a working lunch at a local western restaurant. There were 12 of us, so we went in several cars. Dan and Dittie arrived first to get a table for us. Daniel left Dittie at the table and told him, "I'll let the others know where we are seated."

As we met Dan at the door, Dittie came running out. There was total fear on his face. He took a hold of Dan and tried to pull him along. He said, "We need to leave Dan. They are wearing guns, and guns are bad." Dan tried to explain that the servers are dressed like cowboys and cowgirls and they have fake guns. They don't work. They are toys. Dittie was petrified and not convinced that it was safe. Daniel talked to him for several minutes and he finally came in, but he was not comfortable. He ate, but he watched the wait staff all the time and was glad to be out of there.

Dittie has no upper front teeth. We thought perhaps he was beaten or tortured, but a missionary friend explained it to us. When children begin to get teeth, they pull out the front ones.

Tetanus is very common in Somalia, and there are no Tetanus shots. They take out their teeth so that if they get lockjaw they can feed them, and they won't die of starvation. We tried to get Dittie some teeth, but we all love his big beautiful toothless smile.

Dittie was slowly making progress, but he still had no idea what it meant to be free. Daniel asked him one day, "Dittie, do you know what it means when I say you are free?"

"Yes Dan Boss. I can come to America. I can have a good job and learn English and I have you, Dan."

"Okay Dittie, but it also means you are free to do anything anyone else can do and go wherever you want to go."

That backfired one day, when Dittie followed Dan into the restroom. Dan asked him, Dittie, do you need to use the restroom?"

"No, Dan Boss."

"Okay then. You can wait outside."

When Dan went out of the restroom, there was a long line of men waiting. Daniel asked, "What's going on?" One of the men said, "This big guy said his Dan Boss was in there and we couldn't go in." "I'm sorry," Dan told them, then turned to Dittie and said, "Dittie, we need to talk."

We have learned from Dittie that you can take down the walls that imprison a man, but he will never be truly free until his mind and soul are free. Dittie was not there yet.

Dittie would be over 6 feet tall if he could stand up straight. When he was tortured and beaten, his legs were broken in several places and he walks with a huge limp. He has to sway from side to side to move. For him to run looks very painful.

At first, he never smiled. You could see fear in his large, brown eyes. They darted from one direction to another as if he was expecting to be hit or attacked. He was afraid to be in a group and would run away to be clear of danger.

Because of his huge long legs, clothes did not fit right and hung on his skeleton body. His clothes were all used clothes from a charity. When Christmas came, they gave him a nice gray second-hand suit. He tried so hard to stand up straight because he knew how he looked. I told him he looked very handsome, and for the first time, I saw a smile.

After some time, he began to feel safe. Every morning he would greet me, "Jambo Boss Lady." I returned the greeting, "Jambo (hello), Dittie." It was nice to see him smile.

Do any of us know what it is like to be a slave or to be tortured? Do we appreciate our freedom? Can we as individuals change the world? The answer to all of these questions is probably no. But there are things we can do.

We can share our life and lifestyle with every opportunity. I will never know exactly how we influenced Dittie's life, but I am hopeful it was tremendous. There is one thing I have learned from all of this. When you care about an individual, you also care about their country, and you don't want anything bad to happen to it. That is why when I say my prayers at night I ask God to watch over our special friend and don't let anything bad happen to Somalia. Please God, help each one of us at Daisy Charters and Shuttles to free the mind and soul of our friend Dittie.

Dittie gave much more to us than we ever gave to him.

Thanksgiving is always fun, but what makes it more fun are the international students we've met through transporting the Defense Language Institute (DLI) students that I invite to share Thanksgiving with our family each year. The DLI uses our company for all the DLI students to introduce them to what democracy is in America.

We pick five or six students up early in the morning, so they can help get everything ready to go to my son's house in the country. He has five acres, a horse, several antique cars, fainting goats, skeet shooting, and always a hayride. My grandchildren love it, and even cry at days end because they don't want it to be over yet.

At first, the DLI students are a little shy; they are just not sure what is going to happen. They're from all over the world, and they have never celebrated Thanksgiving before. We have had students from China, Poland, Japan, Arabia, Germany, and Dubai, to name a few.

They often have diet restrictions, so we label all our dishes so the students know exactly what they are eating. We don't eat until later, so as soon as we arrive, the fun begins. They love to put on a cowboy straw hat and ride the horse. They take a joy ride or even drive one of the antique Model T cars, or help the kids build a fort with bales of hay.

When dinner is ready, we all gather around the table to give thanks. They can join us if they want or wait in an adjacent room. Almost always, they join us to give thanks. My then son-in-law would say the prayer. We give thanks for the wonderful year we have had, for all the blessings, for our food, and for our guests and their families. We asked God to watch over them, their families, and bless them with peace. It was obvious that they were touched.

Later we had skeet shooting; a hayride with all the family; and finally, we all cheered on the Dallas Cowboys football game. It was a fun, fun day!

When darkness falls, it is time to go back to the base. It can be an emotional time. One young soldier from Moldova hugged me as he was getting ready to leave. With tears in his eyes, he said, "I will never forget you or your wonderful family. I will remember you always. I have a whole new concept of who Americans are and what America is. I want you to know that every Thanksgiving for the rest of my life, I will think of all of you."

Then he got in the van and was gone. He had taken so many pictures. He was going to send them to his family in Moldova. Now every Thanksgiving I think of him and know he is remembering us.

Daniel was going home one evening when he saw a large black purse fly out of the car ahead of him. He thought it had been left on the roof of the car and forgotten. He stopped, picked up the purse and started putting things back in it. Another car stopped and started to help, but they were putting things in their pocket. When they started to leave with the things they had picked up, Daniel stopped them.

"Leave everything here," he said. "Her bank book is here and has her name and number. I will call her." They were reluctant. "Do I have to call the police?" he asked. "I have your license number." They gave Dan the few things they had retrieved and left.

When Daniel got home, he called the number on the check. A woman answered.

"I found your purse," he said. "I think you left it on the roof of your car and forgot it."

"Oh no!" she said. "Two men snatched my purse and ran away. I was on my way to pay my taxes."

Daniel told her he had it and she could pick it up at Daisy Charters and Shuttles the next day.

"Is there a billfold in it?" she asked.

Daniel looked in the purse. "No, ma'am. I am sorry. I guess they took it and then got rid of the purse."

"Is there a small black change purse in the bottom of the bag?" she asked.

Daniel said, "Let me look. Yes, there is," he told her.

"Is there money in it?" she asked.

Daniel opened it and found a wad of $100 bills. Mrs. Montgomery screamed and started to cry.

"That is the $3,600 to pay my taxes." She was sobbing.

Daniel told her, "Don't cry. Your money is safe. Come by and get it tomorrow. It will be in the safe at Daisy Charters and Shuttles.

Mrs. Montgomery said, "They got my billfold with $25, but an angel found my purse!" She kept "God blessing" Daniel and said she would see him at 8 a.m. the next day.

Daniel gave her his name and address and told her he gets to work at 7 a.m. Morning came and no one showed up. Noon came and went, and still no one. Finally, at 3:30 p.m., a car came into our lot. Daniel was in one of the buses close by. An older African American woman got out, as well as a young girl, obviously her granddaughter.

"Would you be Mrs. Montgomery?" Dan called to her.

"Yes," she said. "Would you be Daniel?"

"Yes, ma'am. I know why you're here."

Again, she began weeping and screaming all at the same time. She was so excited to get her money back that she had forgotten where Daniel worked. All she could remember was that it was on Houston Street. She had been going up and down Houston Street to every business looking for a "Daniel."

Daniel brought them into our office. They could not believe their good luck. Daniel went to the safe and got the purse. "Count your money, Mrs. Montgomery. I want you to be sure that it is all there. I believe you said you had $1,600," he told her.

"No," she said. "I have $3,600, and it is all here."

Mrs. Montgomery was so happy. She wanted to give Daniel a reward. "No," he said. "There's no need for that."

"But I have to give you something," she said.

"Okay," said Daniel. "How about a hug. I like hugs."

Daniel got a bear hug. She turned to me, Daniel's mom.

"This is a fine young man," she said. "His mama raised him right."

I thanked her. Mrs. Montgomery told us how she had just gotten out of the hospital and was on her way to pay her taxes with money she had saved for a year when 2 young men snatched her purse and sped away. There were more tears and hugs before they left the happiest people in the world.

Mrs. Montgomery was the matriarch of the neighborhood, it turns out, and the news spread fast. They called Daniel a hero. They wanted to write up the story for the newspaper, but Daniel said, "No, don't let the robbers know they should check the entire purse before throwing it out."

For weeks, the local merchants treated Daniel with various things. He didn't have to pay for a taco or soda or anything in the neighborhood. The best thing is that we have endeared our company to everyone on the east side. They look out for us and take care of our property. The word is, "Don't mess with Ms. Daisy or Mr. Daniel. They are our kind of people." We don't even get any graffiti anymore. Yea!

Marcos Bonassi came into our lives from a student exchange program when our family decided we would host a student for a year from another country.

It was an easy decision to make. The children thought it would be fun to learn about another country. My husband, Everett, and I wanted to instill in our children the love of travel. There were times later on that we thought maybe we over did it because they travel the world now and love every minute of it.

We passed the exchange student sponsorship examination and were told our student, Marcos Bonassi, would arrive from Sao Paulo, Brazil.

We were very excited as we waited for him at the airport on his arrival day with big signs saying, "Welcome to America, Marcos!" He had studied English before coming, but being immersed was very new. He definitely knew the words Mom, Dad, my "seester" (sister), and my brother.

He was perfect for us, and we knew it immediately. He arrived in July, so we had a few weeks before school started to help him improve his English. We knew coming to San Antonio would change his life, and we wanted his year with us to be an exciting and fulfilling one.

Marcos came from a middle-class family in Sao Paulo. He had two sisters. They lived in a small, four-room house. There were two bedrooms, a kitchen, and a family room. Marcos slept on the couch. These were good, hardworking people doing the best they could for their children. They chose Marcos to come to America for his great academic grades and his desire to be in America for a year.

Marcos would attend his senior year of high school in San Antonio. I went to speak with the counselor assigned to him.

"The first thing we do is work on his English," she said. "The best way to do that is for the entire family to correct any mistake whenever they are talking to him. Can he take it?" she asked.

"I'll ask him," I replied.

Marcos agreed. It would be the fastest and easiest way to learn. We didn't make it a big issue. If he said "seester," we made him say "sister," and he would correct it. The ending "ed" was a big problem for him. Every time he wanted to make a word past tense, he added "ed" to it: look ed, walk ed. "Make it one syllable." we told him. Soon he was catching on, and his English was improving fast.

One day he came running to me. "Mama, Mama," he said. Words failed him. He couldn't find the word he wanted to say.

"Okay, Mom," then he sang, "La Cucaracha, La Cucaracha in the garage!"

That I understood and I went running with a large can of bug spray. A few months later, I was getting our David ready for school, so Marcos left me a note.

"Mom," it said. "This I need. Toothpaste (the minty kind) and soup."

"Okay," I thought. I got the toothpaste and made a big pot of vegetable soup.

When Marcos came home, I presented him with the toothpaste and told him to come to the kitchen. "The soup is vegetable and it's on the stove." He looked at the soup.

"Mama," he said," "I made a big mistake. I need soap, but I eat the soup."

He never got those words mixed up again.

Marcos loved all snack food that was available, anywhere, anytime, especially chocolates. He gained 30 pounds the first 6 months, so we cut back on those things. They do not eat snack food in Brazil, only three meals a day. It would be an adjustment when he went home.

He did well in school. He loved the basketball and baseball games and the dances. He loved it all. We treated him as if he were our own child. If he got in trouble, we scolded him. Sometimes we even grounded him. He never complained. "I was sorry, Mama," he'd tell me.

Marcos loved to watch cartoons because the English was easy to understand, and he learned a lot just listening and watching.

We took him skiing at Christmas. He had never seen snow, and he was thrilled. In the summer, we planned a trip to the Gulf Coast. We had all the gear loaded and we pulled a Volkswagen Thing to drive on the beach.

When we stopped for gas, the five kids got out of the car. The man pumping the gas looked at all of them and said to my husband, "You have a fine family, but only one looks like you."

"Thank you," my husband said. "They mostly look like their mom," and let it go.

Marcos got back in the car. "Are you okay?" I asked him as I got in myself.

"Yes, Mama. I didn't want to speak because I didn't want him to know that I didn't belong to you," he said.

"Well, Marcos," I said. "As far as we are concerned, you do belong to us."

He smiled. "Thank you, Mama."

The year seemed to fly by with Marcos in the midst of it all. He never did anything to have us regret that we had him in our family. We learned so much about Brazil and South America. Marcos would cook his favorite Brazilian food for us from time to time.

He was set to leave us the following July. There were so many things we wanted to talk to him about before he left. One that we worked on for a long time was, "What are you going to do when you go home, Marcos?"

"Well, my uncle has a fabric company, and I can have a job at $5 an hour. That is probably my only option," he said.

"Marcos," we said. "You are much too bright to do that for the rest of your life." We started talking to him about trying for a scholarship to college.

Then we devised a plan to get him acquainted with work in various professions. My sister teaches 1st grade. She took him to school with her one day. My husband arranged for Marcos to observe surgery one Saturday morning. I told him of my plans to start a company and got him involved in business. Finally, we convinced him he should try for a scholarship.

"Okay, Mama," he said. "I'll try for a medical school scholarship. That is the only way I could go to college."

We agreed and worked harder on his English and math. Medical school in Brazil is 6 years. There is a chance, we thought.

The day of departure, we all went to the church. We prayed for all the students that their year in America would be useful to them and it would help them in the years to come. There were tears. It was like losing a son, but I knew there was a mama waiting for him in Brazil who couldn't wait to have him back.

All the exchange students rode the bus from San Antonio to Austin where he would get his flight to return to Brazil. He had presents and pictures galore for all his family. He wrote to me later that the trip to Austin was very quiet, except for the crying. It was hard for the other kids, too.

Before he left, we told him that if he went to medical school, the whole family would come to see him graduate. Marcos arranged to take the medical entrance exam for a scholarship. The day he took it, he called.

"Mom," he said. "The test wasn't that hard. On the English word test, I missed only one word, 'detest.' Why didn't you teach me detest?"

"Because you loved it all, Marcos. You never detested anything!"

Eight hundred students took the test. Forty would be chosen from the first 400, and 40 from the other 400. Marcos made the first cut. In fact, he aced it. He called us thrilled that his family would now have a doctor in it. Marcos did well and went on to become a dermatologist. With what he made, he put his two sisters through school. Whenever he has a meeting or a chance to come to America, he comes to see us.

When he graduated, we took the whole family to Sao Paulo just as we promised. We met his family and friends. We learned to Samba and ate wonderful Brazilian food. The experience was the trip of a lifetime for our family, now numbering eight because our daughters had married.

When people ask, "Did any of your children go into medicine?" I tell them, "Only one. He's a dermatologist in Sao Paulo, Brazil."

Marcos is so proud that his American mom owns a bus company. "That would never happen in Brazil," he'd say. "But it should. My other mom is very capable." He encouraged me every step of the way. He wanted pictures of my office and my fleet so people would believe he had this very successful mom.

Did we make a difference in Marcos's life? I know we did. Not only his, but in his sisters' and his mom and dad's, as well. He bought them a new home they love. Which, Marcos or our family, got the most out of all this? I will tell you, it was our family, because Marcos added so much to all our lives and still does.

Jacob worked on our wash rack. Working the wash rack is a very difficult job. To begin with, the hours are terrible. Whenever a bus returns, we clean it immediately to be ready for the next trip. Sometimes the turnaround time can be after midnight in a very short window of an hour or two. It is very cold work in the winter and boiling hot in the summer. About the only people we can get to work it are people who are desperate for a job.

Because there is a halfway house near our office, we get many newly released ex-convicts. Jacob was such a man. He came in pleading for a job and we hired him.

"I am an ex-con," he said. "Will that upset anyone on the wash rack?"

"No," I told him. "You will fit right in. Most of them are ex-cons, as well."

Jacob had a girlfriend, Lacy, who was on parole for a drug sentence. She was trying hard to get her life straightened out. One day they came to me and said they wanted to start a new life together, clean.

"Great," we said. "We'll do all we can to help."

Lacy had two jobs. One was at night, the other at a restaurant during the day. She was bright and had graduated from college with two degrees, one in computer science and the other in business. She seemed to be trying very hard to get her life together again.

Jacob passed his drug tests and was doing well. We watched both of them like a hawk. They were married on Valentine's Day on the courthouse steps. To show their appreciation for their jobs when no one else would hire them, they came by the office with a beautiful, decorated cake. It was nice to see them staying clean and doing well. The whole office celebrated their wedding.

Lacy had written a poem when she was in prison, and she brought it to me as a gift. The prison paper published it.

"Now, everyone admitted to jail gets a copy," she told me. Lacy was so proud. She had published her first poem.

They worked at Daisy Charters and Shuttles until they made enough money to move to a better apartment in a better part of town. Eventually, they decided to move back to Lacy's home in Florida where they had family who were welcoming them home. She was so proud of herself and of Jacob for being clean, and they gave us all the credit because we gave them a chance. I never heard from them again. I just hope they are doing well.

Chapter 14

Our Family Crisis

My son, Daniel, lives in the country, way out in the country. He has a horse, some dogs, cats, and a fainting goat on 5 acres. In the summer of 2009, our area of Texas had a severe drought. Being in the country, all the wild critters come looking for water.

One evening Daniel heard his dogs barking wildly. He took a flashlight and went to investigate expecting to find a possum. Instead, he heard the rattles of a rattlesnake. He returned to the house and got a shotgun. He went back outside with his flashlight, spotted the snake, and shot it. The 44-inch snake had 12 rattles. It was a very scary experience.

A few days later, one of his neighbors killed two rattlesnakes about the same size. This made Daniel a little edgy, so he always checks on barking dogs.

One night he got up to go to the bathroom. He did not turn on the light as he had lived there for many years. As he went to use the toilet, he felt a sting above his knee. He turned on the light to check it just in time to see a water moccasin going down the toilet. It had obviously come up through the sewer looking for water.

Daniel immediately drove to the ER. The bite was with only one fang and was what they called a dry bite meaning very little venom got into his bloodstream. The doctor checked him over and in a few hours released him. He had a sore leg, but it only lasted a few days.

This particular event made him very cautious. He never got up without turning on the light. One evening he had to replace the batteries in his TV monitor. While he was doing this, one used battery fell on the floor and he thought it rolled under the couch.

Later that night as he went to bed, he crawled in bed and felt a slither feeling down his leg. He threw down the covers, grabbed his 12-gauge shotgun and aimed it at a AAA battery that had obviously dropped into his clothes.

He laughs telling the story on himself. It got him thinking about snakes though, and he decided he needed to move to a more populated area. He put his house up for sale. He didn't know it would just be his first dealing with snakes. There would be more soon.

Daniel was house hunting. He wanted to live in the country, and he found a beautiful brick home in a little town called Floresville just south of San Antonio. Because Daniel has ties to Corpus Christi so often with Daisy Charters and Shuttles, it was perfect because it is on the way to Corpus, reducing his travel time a lot.

Slowly he moved all his furniture into the new home. The only thing left was cleaning the house he had sold. It was evening, and he was almost finished. The only thing he had left to do was bag up some clothes he had thrown into a clothesbasket to drop off at Goodwill. He got a bag and reached for a bundle of clothes. He felt a sting on his finger and he knew immediately. It was another rattlesnake. This time it got him good. He dropped everything, got in his truck and started to the hospital.

En route, he called his dad, who is a doctor. "I'll meet you in the ER," his dad told him. "Leave the phone on. If you feel like you are going to pass out, we will call 911. Meanwhile, let me know where you are. Just call out the milestones."

Daniel reached the ER safely. He walked in and told the nurse, "I've been bitten by a rattlesnake."

"Weren't you here a while back for a snake bite?"

"Yes," Dan replied. "A year ago, almost to the day."

Everett and I arrived. The hospital had no anti-venom on hand, so they started calling around to try to find some. They located some, but said it would be an hour at least before they could get it out to him. Meanwhile, Everett said that he was in good hands, and we needed to go home. Everett had a surgery to perform the next morning, too, so we left.

Shortly after we left, the pain started. Daniel said it was the worst pain he had ever had. He begged for a pain pill. Then he asked for morphine. In desperation, he begged them to cut his finger off. He was in mortal pain. The anti-venom arrived, and they started the treatment. The pain began to subside and Daniel got through the night. In the morning, the doctor came in and marked on Daniel's arm how far the venom was invading. It was a steady move up his wrist to his forearm and beyond, but the pain was better.

Daniel's older sister, Beth, came to see him. She was there when the doctor returned. He told Daniel, "I have good news and bad news. The anti-venom is working. That is good. But, your kidneys and liver are shutting down."

"Okay," Daniel said. "What do we do?"

"Not much," the doctor said. "Just pray."

"Okay," Daniel replied. "Let's see what happens."

"You are taking this very well," the doctor told Daniel.

"Do I have a choice?" replied Dan.

"I think it is time we pray," said Beth, and they did. She asked God to help Dan's kidneys and liver start working again.

God must have heard, because Daniel started getting better. Everything started working, and the line on his arm began to recede. Daniel was in the hospital 3 days. Finally, a specialist was called in. He looked at Daniel and said, "You are good to go. It will take a little time before that line is gone, but you will be fine."

The doctors believe that the first rattlesnake bite gave Daniel some antibodies that helped him through the next one. Whatever it was, Daniel tries to avoid rattlesnakes at all cost.

2008 and 2009 were also critical years for me, personally. It all started when I decided I needed a total knee replacement. I couldn't take the pain any more. It turns out it was one of the easiest things I ever did. I went to the hospital at 5 a.m. on a Tuesday morning and was in surgery by 7 a.m.

That night, I walked to the nurse's station. The next day, I learned how to get in and out of a car and the tub. On Thursday, I practiced what I had learned. On Friday, I went home, and on Monday, I went back to work.

I worked my way through a wheelchair, crutches, a walker, and finally a cane. My spirits were good and that awful pain in my knee was gone. I had therapy 4 mornings a week before going to work, which I hated. However, it had to be done. I forced myself to go. Finally, I was walking pretty well with an arm from anyone close by, but I was just happy I was walking.

When Christmas came a few months later, I felt well enough to do the Christmas Party. It was something I did every year for my employees and friends. I took a week off from work to do all the cooking, and my children helped. It wasn't easy. I made 5 meats, 10 appetizers, 16 side dishes, and 18 desserts. The dessert table started out with 8 desserts, but when one was gone a new and different one appeared. This time, I had the privilege of serving my employees, and it was fun. The party was always at my house. Well, all over my house, yard, and patio. I expected 125 to 140 guests that year.

The night before the party, all was going well. Almost everything was ready. All I had to do was set up the coffee. I had 45 cups of water in my coffee maker, and I was carrying it from the sink to the coffee bar. It was a very short distance, maybe 5 feet, but my foot caught up in a throw rug and I went down. Water went everywhere. My leg hit against the counter, and I knew immediately I had broken my femur. My husband rushed me to the ER and set me up to have surgery.

My girls called me and said, "We're on our way over to the hospital for you to fill us in on all we need to do." My daughter sat beside me in the emergency room taking pages of notes on how to pull it off.

"Everything is ready except the coffee. Fix that and the party will go on."

I had everything organized in a notebook. What food went where? All casseroles were marked with how long to heat them. "It tells you everything," I said. "And even what tables to use and where each dish goes. The party will go on! We will not waste all this food."

They agreed and got busy. There was no doubt in my mind they could do it. That night 128 guests arrived, and by mid party, several people asked, "Where is June?"

Everett gathered everyone in our big family room. He stood on the stairs and told them what had happened and that at that precise moment, I was in surgery. A nurse was keeping him informed as to how I was doing. That's the way I wanted it.

I was so proud of my children. They handled everything "by the book," and everyone had a wonderful time.

At 9:30 p.m., they called Everett to tell him I was in recovery and doing fine. He waited until he was sure I was awake and then came over with all the details about the party.

The femur is the largest bone in the body and takes a long time to heal. The procedure was to put a long titanium rod from my hip to my knee. I got up that night and stood by the bed. I was in the hospital 9 days and had 6 weeks of the dreaded physical therapy. Those 6 weeks were the most miserable days of my life. Then I started the same routine: wheelchair, crutches, walker, and cane. Of all the problems I have had in my lifetime, this was the worst. I thought, "I'd rather have brain surgery." I didn't know it was waiting for me in the wings.

I totally missed Christmas that year. I didn't even get the presents wrapped, but I kept going. "Surely," I thought, "Nothing else can happen. I am well now. I am back, as good as ever." However, I was wrong.

I had noticed for some time that I could not hear very well from my right ear. I went to see several specialists, but they all told me, "You are getting older, and this is normal. When it gets bad enough, we'll give you a hearing aid." For several years, I ignored it.

I sing in the church choir, and I wanted to be able to hear, so I went to see a friend who was a specialist. This time I just said, "I want a hearing aid." He did several tests and said he would call me the next day to set up a fitting.

When he called the next afternoon, I was ready with my calendar to set up an appointment to have the hearing aid fitted. His voice seemed concerned when he said, "June, we found something else that explains your hearing loss. You have a type of tumor called an acoustic neuroma."

I was stunned. "How bad?" I asked. "Can you treat it with chemo or radiation?"

"That won't be necessary," he said. "Acoustic neuromas are noncancerous tumors. They grow on the auditory nerve. Because these tumors are benign, they do not spread to other body parts. You have had it for years. Others just missed it somehow. It's what is causing your hearing loss. While an acoustic neuroma never invades the brain, it can grow large enough to damage important nerves, causing imbalance, headaches, confusion, and difficulty swallowing. If it eventually grew large enough to press on the brain stem, it could cause death. Even though it is extremely slow growing, we need to take care of it. When can we do the surgery?" he asked.

"Tomorrow," I said.

He laughed. "We are not that good," he replied. "We can't get you on the schedule tomorrow, but the next day is fine. We will have to have a neurologist see you first. Also, we'll need a radiation physicist to help."

That afternoon I was in his office. "We could do regular surgery," the doctor said. "However, there is a new procedure using what's called a gamma knife." He went on to tell me how it worked. I'd be in the MRI machine and radiation would be sent to the tumor from hundreds of points. They would all cross over, meet at the tumor, and destroy the blood supply around it. It would take 4 hours, and they could do it tomorrow.

"I am ready. I'll take the gamma knife. No need to tell the kids. They have had enough of my problems."

I went into the hospital the next morning at 5 a.m. and had 6 sessions in the MRI tube with my head screwed into a helmet so I wouldn't move. I'd like to say it was easy, but it wasn't. It was scary. The radiation physicist measured the amount of radiation I needed. I prayed and tried to be a good patient.

By 10:30 a.m. I was finished, and I walked out under my own power. I was left with a severe hearing loss in my right ear, but 6 months later, another MRI showed the tumor to be half-gone and dying.

Had I known what was in store for me during that 18-month period, I would have given up. But God is good. He gave me strength to keep on fighting. Two years later, there is only a trace of the tumor left. Next year it will be gone.

The tumor was bad, but the broken femur was 10 times worse. I'll take an acoustic neuroma anytime. I went to see our ear, nose, and throat specialist. He treated me with two small hearing aids that work great. Now my left ear talks to my right ear, and I hear very well. No one even notices my hearing aids.

Today I am as good as ever with only a few scars to show for my 18-month endurance test. I am one of the lucky ones. Everything I had could be treated, as long as I didn't give up. And I don't give up – ever!

The only problem now is when I go to the airport; I light up like a new saloon.

I've grown accustomed to the pat down.

Chapter 15

Achievements, Awards, and Recognition

I have always been competitive. I was born into it. I had two sisters, one older and one younger. Being the middle child, I had many challenges. Early on I noticed that my older sister got to do many things because she was the oldest (like being boss when mom and dad were not there), and my younger sister got allowances because she was the baby.

Where did that leave me? No man's land. I tried at every opportunity to exceed so I could be boss or best at something. It was good for me because it made me into a competitive giant, and I know it helped me in the years ahead. Even to this day, if I am in a competitive situation, I try my best to be at the top.

There have been many awards along the way. The recognition has been good, but the way I look at it is this: it has been great publicity and costs nothing at times when my funds were very limited. The following are a few of my favorite awards and achievements.

1953 Registered Nurse, Huron Road Hospital in association with Western Reserve University

1958 First Woman to solo fly for her pilot's license at Randolph AFB Flying Club

1980 Designed "How to Organize For Political Action" for American Medical Association

1987 First Recipient of the Belle Chenault Award for Excellence in Political Action

1996 Industry Transportation Woman of the Year

1998 Greater San Antonio Chamber Small Business Leader of the Year

2000 Entrepreneurial Spirit Award – Benefactor Category NAWBO

2001 Destination Magazine article, "A Motherly Touch."

2004 San Antonio Chamber Overall Outstanding Business Leader of the Year

2006 Entrepreneurial Star – Women of Diversity (1 of 3 per year)

2006 National Association of Women Business Owner of the Year

2007 Daisy Charters and Shuttles on the cover of Bus Ride Magazine

1999, 2001, 2007 SDDC Quality Award, Lackland AFB-USAF

2006, 2007, 2008 Honorary Base Commander 345th Training Squadron USAF

2008 Go Red For Women local chapter chairman

2008 Entrepreneurial Spirit Award – NAWBO

2008 National Association of Professional and Executive Women – Woman of the Year, A Woman of Excellence

2010 Daisy Charters and Shuttles picked as one of San Antonio's Top 50 Companies

My American Medical Association friend, Belle Chenault, said this:

"June dares to dream and makes dreams come true for all of us."

Daisy Charters and Shuttles has been privileged to win the SDDC (Surface Deployment and Distribution Command) Quality Award from the Federal Government. It is awarded for outstanding service to the US military worldwide. We are the only bus company ever to win the award, and we've won it three times. We've joined the ranks of other winners, which include prominent airlines, shipping companies, and oil and gas companies.

Below is the letter Lt. Col. David A. Hasse submitted when he nominated Daisy Charters and Shuttles for the award.

2007 SDDC Quality Award Nomination
Daisy Tour Service Summary

Daisy Charters and Shuttles has proven to be a reliable partner with Lackland AFB in its mission as "Gateway to the Air Force." "Quality" is the only way to describe this bus company. Daisy's safety record is flawless – 1.3 million accident-free miles in the past year. They scored a "One" on their 2006 SDDC Safety Inspection – the 4th year in a row – Outstanding!

As a result of their reputation, reliability, and outstanding safety record, Daisy Charters and Shuttles was selected as Lackland's primary carrier in support of the Basic Military Training (BMT) mission, delivering virtually all 38,000 USAF recruits to Lackland AFB in 2006. Following graduation 6 weeks later, the USAF entrusted Daisy Charters and Shuttles to transport an average of 15 buses weekly, with every single bus on time, with a fully qualified, dedicated driver.

In addition to Daisy's record of safety, reliability, and responsiveness, they saved USAF over $6 million by avoiding commercial air travel for 22,727 BMT graduates to their technical training schools in Mississippi and Texas.

Among Lackland's unique training missions is the DoD Working Dog Center. Daisy Charters and Shuttles went the extra mile to transport military working dogs and their handlers by removing bus seats to accommodate kennels for an air-conditioned, round trip from Lackland AFB to Yuma, Arizona. Mission accomplished!

Another unique mission is USAF Basic Combat Convoy Course (BC3). Soldiers are organized and trained to operate as army truck companies and then deployed to provide convoy protection in Iraq. After 6 weeks of intense training at Camp Bullis in San Antonio, Texas, they airlift them to Ft. Sill, Oklahoma, for heavy weapons training. By using Daisy's buses for this move, the DoD saved $120,000 versus MilAir. Also, importantly, these warriors only had to load/unload their bags and equipment once – eliminating four additional manual lifting of 13 short tons at the origin and destination airfields. They arrived fed, fresh, and ready for field training and subsequent deployment to a combat zone.

Daisy's owner and staff are active members of San Antonio Chapter of the National Defense Transportation Association (NDTA); their tireless efforts helped earn Chapter of the Year honors for 2006. They helped raise and award $3,500 in local scholarships and donated an additional $500 to NDTA's national scholarships. The chapter annually sorts more than 20 tons of donated food for the San Antonio Food Bank. They also served a meal to the residents of Wilford Hall Medical Center's Fisher House, where the families of the wounded and seriously ill can be close to their recovering warriors.

The commanding general, 37th Training Wing, recognized June Bratcher, Daisy Charters and Shuttles' owner, as Honorary Commander for the 345th Training Squadron, USAF's Transportation Schoolhouse, in appreciation of her outstanding contributions to San Antonio's military community.

Without question, Daisy Charters and Shuttles' emphasis on safety, customer service, responsiveness, and reliability has earned the SDDC Quality Award for service in our nation's defense.

Lt. Col. David A. Hasse

To be featured on the cover of your industry magazine is a real honor. BUSRide Magazine always has a bus on their cover, so only 12 of the 1,100 United Motor Coach companies have that honor each year.

I became acquainted with the editor of BUSRide Magazine, David Hubbard, when he featured a short article about Daisy Charters and Shuttles in 2001. I really liked him and his article and look forward to the magazine every month. I hoped someday to meet him.

We were very surprised when he called one day and said he wanted to feature Daisy Charters and Shuttles on the cover of the September 2007 issue of BUSRide Magazine. What an opportunity! We hired a photographer and took several photos around San Antonio. The one that we finally decided on was in front of the sports complex where San Antonio's professional basketball team plays.

The name of the article in the magazine was, "A woman's touch," and it was perfect. What a proud day it was when the magazine came out. We got calls from all over the country. "How did you land that?" or "How did you pull that off?" were typical questions. Only one caller said, "No woman-owned bus company should ever be on the cover of BUSRide Magazine. Buses are a man's job." By now, I was accustomed to these kinds of remarks, and I let it go.

Lots of industry people called, emailed, and even sent flowers to congratulate us. We were so proud. I finally met Mr. Hubbard at a United Motor Coach Industry National Conference, and he was every bit as nice as I thought he would be.

The following pages are his article from 2006.

BUSRide Article 2006. – Reprinted with consent of David Hubbard

A woman's touch
June Bratcher leads Daisy Tours-Conventions San Antonio

The company Motto, "We can do that," pours directly from the president and founder of Daisy Tours-Conventions San Antonio, June Lee Bratcher.

Bratcher launched her career in the bus business in 1980 on the heels of a nursing career that supported her husband, Everett, through medical school. Wanting more productive time at home, she recognized a need to help friends and associates with travel for sightseeing and functions throughout San Antonio. Starting with $200.00 and doing the work free of charge, her activities soon took over nearly every room in the house.

Today Daisy Tours-Conventions San Antonio operates a fleet of 18 Van Hool motorcoaches, employs 36 people and produces upward of $4.2 million in annual sales. This past June the National Association of Woman Business Owners honored Bratcher as its 2006 Women Business Owner of the Year.

Bratcher originally intended to start Bluebonnet Tours, but her restricted budget only allowed stationary from WalMart. With a daisy pattern her only choice she simply changed the name.

"Daisy Tours worked so well my husband told me I had to either go into business or get out because this was consuming my life," says Bratcher. "When I told my friends I had to give it up, they said all I had to do was charge. I started figuring my costs and adding a percentage and it began to fall together for me."

Bratcher says in a short time she moved operations into her first office away from home.

"It was small but still lent a more professional feel, "she says. "From that point I knew I could grow the business, but I ran into a wall." She says every bank refused her loan requests unless her husband co-signed. "He offered, I refused," says Bratcher. "I felt a woman should be able to get a loan on her own. After working so many years to put him through medical school, internship and residency, I wanted this as mine alone."

Seven years after starting the business, Bratcher attended a government sponsored program for women in business. For her class project she compiled a 37-page loan package that she could take to her bank. "By this time, bankers were tired of seeing me coming," she recalls. "This time, they were hesitant as usual, but my thoroughness surprised them, and especially when I told them I had prepared this request on my own. Calling her presentation "textbook quality," they extended Daisy Tours-Conventions San Antonio $125,000 to jump fully into the bus business. She purchased her first motorcoach – an older used MCI – From Kerrville Bus, and bought three more in a short succession through a subsequent loan from the Small Business Association.

Franklin Roe, a longtime driver and all-around busman with Kerrville helped Bratcher with her first vehicles. Once he retired, he came onboard as partner in Daisy Tours to oversee fleet operations.

In 1997, they purchased the former Greyhound property and were able to locate the offices and bus maintenance facilities in one central location. "Our first coaches were in great condition and very well maintained," says Bratcher. "Still, the older model buses really hurt our image. I would hear comments like, "Daisy buses are clean, Daisy buses arrive on time, but they are old." Even with our new Van Hools, it has taken a long time to rid the business of the stigma of running older buses.

Bratcher purchased her first new bus from ABC Companies in 1998.

"Greg Gates, our ABC Companies sales representative in Grand Prairie, TX was the first to show me a way to purchase new coaches," says Bratcher. "I was never aware of the financing options that he pointed out --- a lease trac with a balloon on the end, which I could also refinance if necessary. I was crazy about Van Hools and ABC created an opportunity for me to move up."

Bratcher says because she could see her business growing, she felt her first purchase of a new Van Hool would not be a tremendous risk.

"Additionally, I am most appreciative of the staff at ABC Companies in Fairbault, MN, and the Van Hools in Belgium for the interest they take in assisting small women-owned businesses," she says. "Everyone from the top down saw to the special coaching I needed to properly manage this important step in the growth of my company."

To protect the hard-earned image of Daisy Tours, Bratcher now operates a coach no longer than six years before putting it up for sale. She says her corporate and convention clients require newer vehicles even though the older models still look good and run well. Bratcher says she will cap the fleet at 20 motor coaches. "It used to be no one could tell the age of a motorcoach," she says. "Now they can and it makes a difference in how we do business. Daisy Tours focuses on three areas of business conventions, military and professional sports.

Conventions San Antonio

Daisy Tours' early bus business relied heavily on school transport. Bratcher faced her first serious business in 1986 when the Texas Legislature passed the No Pass, No Play law. Bratcher says the legislation severely reduced the number of school field trips and extracurricular travel, and caused a 40.5 percent drop in projected earnings for Daisy Tours.

To counteract the situation, she re-grouped with her staff and developed Conventions San Antonio to further diversify. "I saw a full-service convention planning business filling the buses, and the bus component enhancing our convention service." "The timing was right to capitalize on the city's massive development to attract more convention business."

Daisy Tours answers the call

The San Antonio economy rests solidly on the U.S. military bases that dot the city map. Once Daisy Tours acquired its first transport contracts with Lackland AFB the company soon became the official carrier. Daisy Tours currently serves five military contracts that extend over the next five years. A few years ago, the Air Force slashed its recruitment quota, which drastically reduced the number of troop transports. This time Bratcher and her staff met the crisis by calling in the National Guard.

"The situation in Iraq was heating up, so we put the word out to National Guard units in every surrounding state that we had buses available for deployments," says Bratcher. "A few days later, we received our first call from El Paso for six buses to Arizona. Soon after that, the other Texas National Guard units started calling.

Bratcher says since then the Air Force bounced back and the National Guard is still a regular customer. As a member of the National Defense Transportation Association, Bratcher was instrumental in convincing the military to consider the quality of the equipment and personal service before merely settling on the lowest bid. As a result, Daisy Tours is now the preferred military transport in San Antonio.

Daisy Tours' biggest fans.

Bratcher's passion for sports has given rise to Daisy Tours' reputation for quality sports transportation. She says she cornered this niche by lobbying for Daisy Tours at NBA trainer meetings, where she also picked up business from the Dallas Mavericks. "It's all about the service and personal touches we provide," says Bratcher. "There's more to it than just driving a bus around. The same driver is on every trip and is in many ways one of the team. In fact, one team left us and came back because management was so insistent on riding only with Rafael, the driver from Daisy Tours."

When Franklin Roe passed away a year ago, Bratcher gathered her four adult children and discussed selling the business. Their feeling was their mom had worked too hard too long to build the business and saw no reason to let it go.

The upshot was her two sons, David and Daniel, dropped their respective positions in advertising and landscape design to carry on with the business. A final note to Bratcher's "can do" spirit. While she was the first woman to solo a small plane at Randolph Flying club, she does not drive buses. "Part of Franklin's legacy, I think was to keep me from behind the wheel," she says. "I wanted to, but he explained to me the guys really needed something that I didn't try to do myself."

BR

In 2005, my friend Blanca Welborn nominated me for the National Association of Women Business Owners (NAWBO) Woman of the Year award. I immediately told her I didn't want the nomination. "There is no way I could win. I couldn't even get a loan for 7 years. I don't want to disappoint my friends at NAWBO."

"We are going to do it anyway," they said. "We are all proud of you already."

At the National Conference in 2006, NAWBO named me Woman of the Year. My NAWBO chapter was thrilled. I was amazed. It was the first time anyone in my chapter had won a national honor, and it really got us in the news. My husband and I flew to San Francisco for the award ceremony. It was an exciting and awesome weekend.

That award opened many doors for us. Newspapers nationwide picked up the story. My hometown newspaper got news of it, and that small town of 1,100 in Ohio celebrated. It is no wonder my high school senior class of 18 named me "most likely to succeed."

At the same time, I was nominated for and won the Entrepreneurial Star Award by the Women's Business International Magazine and joined six other women in Washington, D.C., in October of that same year. It was amazing. I thought, "This little old farm girl from Ohio, to be with such accomplished women." It was hard to believe.

"Go Red For Women, the American Heart Association's national movement to end heart disease and stroke in women, was one of my favorite endeavors. It was something I could put my heart into. I really believed in their cause. So when a Go Red For Women executive came by my office and said they wanted me to chair the 2008 drive to raise funds, I couldn't say no.

I knew it would be hard, but I said, "Yes, let me try." We didn't set a goal. Instead, we said, "Let's see how much we can raise."

I met every Monday morning with a Go Red For Women executive member and told her what my plans were. She would go over everything with me and advise me on the best way to do the things I had planned. All through the week, I would follow up on those plans. I had established a great committee; the members were hard working and enthusiastic about what we were doing. I hit the big spenders first—those who would find it easy to give $20,000 to $30,000.

I called people who were my very best customers, like ABC Companies, who sold me all of my buses. They agreed to take a bus and put Go Red For Women decals all over it. It was beautiful and we used it all over San Antonio and Texas. On our celebration day, they sent two of their employees to the luncheon. They came from Faribault, Minnesota, so it was an expensive matter, but a true, "I want to help" event.

Doctors' wives are good for a $5 donation for anything, so I sent letters to all of them regularly. I carried donation cards with me all the time and gave them out to people I thought should help. I gave the Red Dress Pin to them so they could show their support of Go Red For Women. Whether anyone gave me a dollar or a dime, I was grateful for anything.

I wanted to do a good job, and I put my heart into it night and day. It was not easy for me because I was still recovering from a broken femur and often had to have help to get around.

On the day of our Go Red For Women celebration lunch, I had to be helped to the stage. I didn't want to need the help, but it had been a long year. I had worked and I was tired, and I didn't want to miss it now that it was coming to an end.

I walked to the microphone on the arm of the local Go Red For Women director. I thanked my fantastic committee and presented my check, which exceeded $200,000. I was very proud of my committee.

Our hard work had paid off, and when heart disease in women is finally conquered, we will know we had a hand in it.

Chapter 16

Moving To the Next Level

In the fall of 2008, we noticed we were getting a lot of business from Corpus Christi on the Gulf Coast. It is a small town about 147 miles from San Antonio. There were three small bus companies there, but they only did casino runs. Schools, churches, and businesses were calling us for transportation services.

The more we did, the more business from Corpus Christi came pouring in. Their Convention and Visitors Bureau called urging us to open a branch there. Daniel took the lead to investigate. They offered us a package deal that included a list of conventions currently booked at area hotels and access to all conventions booked into Corpus Christi for the next few years.

When Daniel and David, my sons, took our coaches down for the Corpus Christi Convention and Visitors Bureau to look at, the bureau was amazed. Their first question was, "Does the AC work?" Then, "Does the restroom work? After David assured the group that everything worked, they begged us to come.

Daniel and David went to look for space to rent. Meanwhile, our business there was growing by leaps and bounds. We found an excellent manager. He could drive a coach, wash them, make sales calls, and generally run the business. George was a lifesaver.

He had worked for two great international tour companies. He assured us he could manage everything.

On April 1, 2009, we ordered two new coaches. We had to ask for delayed delivery, as we had no place to park them. Finally, we took two of the coaches we owned to Corpus Christi and sent two drivers to Florida to pick up the two new ones. Our buses come from Belgium. They are Van Hool coaches. They must be quarantined for a week before we can pick them up.

To say opening an office in Corpus Christi was scary is putting it mildly. We were sticking our neck out again. We put all the precaution in it that we could. We had a 6-month property lease on the office space. In San Antonio, we started booking coaches for Corpus Christi as well as Laredo, Texas, and all along the Gulf Coast. We already had several Corpus Christi conventions booked and even had to send San Antonio coaches to cover the overflow.

Daniel is pretty much in charge of our Corpus Christi office, and he does a great job. He got us involved as a sponsor for The Tall Ships that were coming in. He joined the Convention and Visitors Bureau, the Chamber of Commerce and their Leadership Corpus Christi. Fortunately, Daniel doesn't know a stranger and made lots of friends. Today we have an office, a yard, office staff, and a driving crew to manage everything. It has proven to be a good investment for us, and this year we will add two more coaches to the fleet in Corpus Christi. Our problem currently is that we still don't have enough coaches there to cover all the requests.

Our coaches now proudly say San Antonio and Corpus Christi. We've been invited to open an office in Dallas. We'll see. Right now, we are really happy to be a part of Corpus Christi. They have welcomed us with open arms.

Many have asked what I did to be so successful. The one thing that has hit home to me time and time again is this: Be financially responsible.

You don't have to have $25,000 worth of office furniture to start. I had a kitchen table, the yellow pages, and an old manual typewriter that my husband had in college.

Don't misunderstand. We have a beautiful office now, but we got it one step at a time when we could afford it. Many entrepreneurs make this mistake. They get a beautiful office, new furniture, state-of-the-art equipment, and expensive staff with all the right credentials. Then they open their doors to a surprise. No one has been waiting for that company to come along.

When I started, for every five businesses men started, one was successful. For every five businesses women started, four were successful for that very reason. Too many men are head over heels in debt before they open their fancy address doors.

Women are more patient. Like me, they start in their home. They establish a great base that will pay the bills, and they keep that base. If one customer falls by the wayside, they quickly replace them, and they are always on the lookout for new customers to be part of their base.

Paying your bills is another clue. It is a temptation, when money comes rolling in, to spend it on all kinds of things. Avoid the temptation, because eventually employees and bills have to be paid.

We always pay our expenses first, no matter how much it hurts. Nothing is marked "profit" until all bills are paid. And, if we see a slow period coming, we put money aside to be sure our bills can be paid.

I have seen so many tour companies fail because they spent their income before all their bills were paid. It is so easy to do. You always think there will be more coming in tomorrow. We must be accountable, tighten our controls, and improve our collections first. Poor financial management has caused many companies to fail when they did not have to.

There are other things that are important to business: the right location, the proper business plan, the right pricing, the right employees and consultants. It is very easy when business is good and collections are booming to feel confident and that it will go on forever.

Never assume because this year is good, next year will be also. I can tell you, it won't. There are things that happen, like 911 or hurricanes or strikes. Never live for the moment. Always plan ahead. Look at the direction the city is going. How much money is coming in? How much will be available in loans? Most importantly is to be able to back up what we say we can do with our performance and doing more than is expected.

We try very hard to make our customers feel like they are our only customers and that they are the most important people in the world, which they are. They are the people who make our company possible.

In the end, you will find you have suffered a little, but the fun times far outweigh the bad. Believe me, you look at a business differently when you run it rather than just work there. It's like one of your children. You give it your life, nurture it, and watch it grow. Finally, someday you stand back, look at it, and say, "It is good. It is just what I always dreamed it would be."

In a few short years, it will be time for me to retire. Not that I want to, but my body is telling me, "Slow down, girl. You can't do what you have always done." I know that I will have to plan for it. I love my company. I never wanted to sell it. Who would take care of it like I do? No one!

We have four children: two girls and two boys. I called them together recently to see how they felt about mom's company.

I told them that after much thought, I had come up with three proposals regarding Daisy Charters and Shuttles.

I can't do this forever so . . .

1. I can sell it and give you the money.
2. I can get someone to run it for you and you get the profit.
3. You can come in and run it as I have all these years, it will be yours.

They said they would think about it. A few days later, they returned. They had met and come to a conclusion. They would try running it for 2 years, and if they liked it, they would stay. If not, they would go to option 1 or option 2.

They elected David as President, Daniel as Vice President, Kim as Vice President in charge of international sales, Beth as Secretary, and my heart was pounding. David is the youngest, the baby. Could he handle it? I held my tongue for a minute.

"Mom," they said. "We know what you are thinking. David is the youngest. Can he handle it? You have to trust us, mom. You have to believe in us." I remained silent.

Today, they are all fully involved with Daisy Charters and Shuttles and loving it as much as I do. David is perfect for president, and Daniel, who has always loved cars and motors, is perfect to manage the garage.

Transferring it to them required some planning and especially some money. Daisy had to be evaluated wealth wise. How much were they getting? Who would get what? How would it be divided? We hired a lawyer, which was good because there was a lot more to it than just signing it over to them.

As we speak, they are now the proud owners. They told me, "Mom, this company is too good to just let it go!" They get along like peas in a pod. They can disagree without getting mad and are doing a wonderful job. The business is growing.

I have gone from CEO to Mom to Chairman of the Board. I believe I can freely say that the "Mom" title out ranks everyone! At least while I am still here.

I am still looking out for my dream, just without all of the little crises along the way. I still get paid. They are good planners, and I love that they also have a great business sense.

They seem to know when to forge ahead and when to back off. They have added so much to the company, like computers. I always thought they were too complicated for my simple mind. Somehow they got it through my head, and even I use a computer now.

I have no fear of leaving for retirement. I know Daisy Charters and Shuttles is in good hands. What is nice is I see a lot of me in their decisions.

"The apple doesn't fall far from the tree."

Chapter 17

A Message to Entrepreneurs

What is an entrepreneur? The dictionary defines entrepreneur as one who organizes, manages, and assumes the risks of a business or enterprise. Do you have an idea or a dream that is entrepreneurial? Here are some guiding ideas.

1. There is no simple path. Look for one you love.
2. Be aware that your goal may change over the years. I started as a cooking school. I never dreamed of a bus company.
3. It is okay to be afraid. Sometimes I was terrified. What if it doesn't work? Reorganize and start over.
4. Failure should not be in your vocabulary. Retreat and reorganize if you have to, but don't give up.
5. Start out with a fallback plan in case you need it. Mine was nursing. If I failed, I could reorganize, work as a nurse to pay off my debt, and then start over with new vigor.
6. Get a partner. Someone who has the skills that you lack. Two heads are always better than one.

7. Remember that you cannot always control everything.
8. Use your imagination. You'll see opportunities others miss.
9. Love what you are doing. If you don't, your business will fail.

Printed in the United States
By Bookmasters